# From Rim Shots
## to Results With....

# SLAM DUNK MARKETING

By Phil "Zoom" Roberts
and Christopher O'Donnell

# CONTENTS

## ACKNOWLEDGMENTS

Thanks to all our colleagues for their invaluable contributions and inspiration. Specifically: Robert Barach and Lloyd M. Wirshba from American Express; Jim Doherty, *Nation's Restaurant News* magazine; Charlie Forman, *Cheers* magazine; Steve Raabe, *The Denver Post*; Herman Cain, Dick Rivera, Skip Sack, Ken Zankell, Rick Van Warner, Hal Smith, Bill Nelson, Kristen Loop, Kristin Kirkland, Bill Asbury, Laurie Uttich, Andrea Stewart, Teri Merbach, Ian Hardin, Julie Eiss, Katie Jensen, Melodye Spurrier, Peggy McDonald, Steve Alderman, Stephen Edwards, Doug Futz, Deborah Henckel, Debbie Snow, Heather Brown, Karin McMillen, Andy Roberts, Jan DiMarco, Doc Gardner, Marti Long, Trish O'Donnell, Liza Mason, Stephanie Blocher, Patrick Friedauier, Darren Minich, Gail Williams, Diane Black, Dana Orme, Mary O'Donnell, Mike Plancarte, Ross Billows, Trina Wamsley, Renée Medina, Leslie Marasco, John Ziegler, Lene Thorud, Bob Bucciarelli, John Jordan and Phoebe Johnson. We would also like to thank all the various business owners, operators and managers who, over the years, contributed their valuable ideas to this book.

## FOREWORD

If you like great marketing ideas that are easy to learn and execute and want to super-charge your own business' profits, you are now reading the right book, at the right time, to get the right results, right here, right now.

Great stories are fun and effective ways to learn, and *Slam Dunk Marketing* is a fun, effective and great story!

One of the keys to business mastery is to model the masters. My dear friend, Zoom Roberts, and his colleague, Christopher O'Donnell, have mastered the fine art of how to execute all sorts of marketing ideas for any business. These easily executed ideas lead to maximum profit creation and more fun while managing your business. You'll learn all about how to do it all in this best-selling book. Drink deeply of their combined marketing wisdom and share it with everyone on your business team. Your results will soar and you'll energize your customers, your staff, your investors, and yourself. Most importantly, your bottom line will shoot through the roof!

Wow yourself! Start by reading this book with a colleague. Discuss how you can systematically implement all the nifty ideas, principles, techniques and strategies to instantly improve your current business operation and future marketing opportunities. *Slam Dunk Marketing* with its simplistic but unique theories and easily executable guidelines quite simply gets results. Christopher and Zoom give you priceless marketing knowledge they've tested daily in their own successful businesses. Their customers almost always become clients, friends and perpetual repeaters and referring fans. Exactly what every business wants.

Before Zoom and I became friends and business associates, I anonymously ate at one of his restaurants. One of the tiny marketing ideas that enhanced the environment at Marlowe's (one of Premier Ventures' great restaurants in downtown Denver) impressed me immensely. Signed photos on the wall of famous customers like Bill Cosby aren't totally unique to celebrity-frequented restaurants. But when the manager at Marlowe's humbly requested that *I* autograph my photo to be placed on the same wall, I cheerfully did so. I now tell everyone I know who is traveling to Denver to go to Marlowe's to see my photo. Wow. Slam Dunk word of mouth.

Their marketing wisdom includes taking photos of the server or manager with their new customer referring client and sending this photo to the client in an ultra-cool magnetic frame that can be slapped up on the client's refrigerator or office file cabinet as a constant reminder of where to return to eat. Many of their best customers invest (not spend – *invest*) in good food, atmosphere and unsurpassed service, and they get a memorable, delightful, return on their investment, and these customers return repeatedly.

As an owner of seven varied super-successful businesses, I know that dollars go where they are invited, and stay where they are welcome. In *Slam Dunk Marketing*, Zoom and Christopher show you how to invite and welcome customers who positively and exuberantly both spend their dollars and spread that priceless asset, great word-of-mouth marketing, that will build and continue to build any business. To learn how to apply *Slam Dunk Marketing* so you capture more happy customers who will love and refer your business to everyone they see and to skyrocket all your future earning power, read, memorize and apply these ideas now!

**Mark Victor Hansen, Co-author of *Chicken Soup for the Soul*, No. 1 New York Times Best-selling Series**

*"It's not necessarily any one big thing you do, it's a combination of the little things that add up to success."*

## CHAPTER 01

Let's get one thing straight. You don't need to be a basketball fan to reap the benefits of reading *Slam Dunk Marketing*. You just need to be a business owner, operator or manager interested in spending less money but getting more profitable results out of your marketing efforts. More for less — that's what this book is all about.

Why *Slam Dunk*? Well, for one thing, it's a high-percentage shot. Basketball players who can dunk the ball without a miss during a game will probably convert only four — maybe five — out of 10 shots launched away from the basket. The other six will miss the mark. Could you afford a 40-to-50-percent success rate on your marketing promotions? More likely, you're aiming and hoping for a slam dunk. A sure thing. A winner as often as possible.

This book's for you. You'll learn the *Slam Dunk Marketing* principles along with Dean, a former college basketball player who now runs a casual-theme restau-

1

rant called the Red River Grill. Nice place, good burgers, but not doing the level of business its proprietor had envisioned when he opened the place. As you'll find out, the secret to building traffic and outdoing the competition has been within Dean's grasp — and yours — all along.

Read this book as if you're on the wing of a fast break, not stopping until you've scored. Early on, some of the code words Dean jots in his Marketing Notebook may seem secretive to you. Fear not — they'll be revealed at the end of the book in the "Dean's Official Marketing Notebook" section, where the 10 steps to *Slam Dunk Marketing* success crystallize in easy-to-implement form.

Turn your marketing shots into slam dunks. Just pick up the ball and go for it.

Phil "Zoom" Roberts              Christopher O'Donnell

© Pencom International • 800-247-8514

— *"Let's not tell anybody about this place.*
*It'll be our secret."*

4

# CHAPTER 1
## WHAT'S WRONG HERE?

My name's Dean. You don't know me personally, but you might know something about what I've been through, especially if you're a business owner, operator or manager not reaching the level of success you'd like to be reaching.

I own and operate the Red River Grill, a casual-theme restaurant known for its wide selection of unique brews and charbroiled burgers. Inside is about 3,000 square feet of dining area, including a horseshoe bar that features the tap handles of 12 craft beers — "microbrews" as they're often called. Cushioned booths line the walls, with four-tops and several deuces set up in the middle. We're open for lunch and dinner every day of the week, catering to small businesses in the area and the students and faculty of the nearby university. The decor has the feel of a riverfront pub or tavern — a mix of wood and brass, antique river-running paraphernalia and a 250-pound tarpon stuffed

5

and hung on the wall, the biggest fish I ever caught on a fly.

All in all, it's a fun place to eat. On the menu you'll find 10 different burgers, ranging from the pineapple-topped "Hawaiian" to the double-decker "Hoss," smothered in cheddar and bacon strips. All are served on toasted buns we make ourselves. We also sell a lot of build-your-own mini-pizzas and grilled-chicken items, including salads, sandwiches and quesadillas. Our "Fire in the Pit Chili" won a blue ribbon at the State Fair a few years back, dethroning the *chili con carne* of the former champion, Bubba Sinclair, who blamed his undoing on a widely spread rumor that he used fresh road kill in his recipe. I hated to resort to that tactic, but all's fair in love and chili cook-offs.

Employees come and go, but I've held together a hardworking, though often wacky, nucleus. My best server, Jessie, has made a career of sparring with guests, but it's all in jest and has been a big hit among the business people who come in for lunch and after work. One of her standard opening lines: "You must feel like the devil because you look like hell."

Then there's Sid behind the bar, a struggling comedian whose William F. Buckley-style jokes and delivery have not caught on with any large audiences yet. Snubbed by most of the clubs that have open-microphone nights, he's finally contemplating a career change. Meanwhile, he's doing a bang-up job, running a tight ship, helping out with the ordering and receiving, and discussing with guests the absurdity of national and local political events.

6

Sharing the cooking duties are Alberto, Ben and Charlie — the ABC crew, for short. I couldn't be happier not only with their food-preparation skills, but also with the way they get involved in developing menu ideas. Our sandwiches come with regular fries or, for a little extra, curly fries seasoned with a secret blend of spices, an idea the ABC crew dreamed up. Our hand-battered, dark-beer onion rings — another ABC inspiration — are the world's best and unlike any other rings in town.

My right-hand man is a woman, though she'd punch me in the nose if I ever called her that in person. Kate's been with me from the beginning, which says something about her intelligence, perseverance or masochistic sense of humor. I'm not sure which. We rotate days off — when there's time for a day off — and split many of the management functions. The budgets we operate under are very tight.

These characters and others have stuck with me through thick and thin, long before I stumbled onto the *Slam Dunk Marketing* principles that would dramatically turn around the fortunes of the Red River Grill. Early on in this venture, the outlook was not nearly as rosy as it is today.

Using my own savings and investments from friends and family, I originally bought and renovated the restaurant five years after working my way up the corporate ladder to a middle-management position at a Fortune 500 company, one of the most successful of its kind. With my experience and education in business, I figured running a restaurant would come

7

as naturally to me as playing basketball did when I started at guard for the local college basketball team. When Coach heard the news, he thought I was nuts. "A restaurant?" he asked. "What do you know about running a restaurant?"

Apparently, not enough. In the years to come, I managed to make a profit, taking home a decent salary. But growth was as slow as a West Texas turtle in August. I couldn't justify opening more restaurants, which has been a goal of mine since I first plunged into this business. I knew from the start what I was getting into — the long workdays, rising costs, chronic turnover and competition at every corner, not to mention a long list of other daily challenges. What I hadn't expected was the difficulty in attracting customers and, more important, *keeping* them.

For insight, I turned to many of the restaurant-management and general-business "how-to" books. The formula often presented — good product + good service = repeat business — seemed entirely within the grasp of an educated and well-trained businessperson like myself. In the real world, however, the Grill produced good food and service, but the repeat business part of the equation didn't take care of itself. You have to get customers in the door to try your product before you can even think about getting them to return. I took a crack at everything short of blackmail to generate new traffic, but too many of the promotions — happy hours, coupon schemes, special offers, TV and radio ads, direct mail and the like — came off as flat as last night's beer.

One day, during a lunch shift, I reached the breaking point. Sitting at the bar, I was practicing every good bartender's primary learned skill — eavesdropping — when I overheard a conversation taking place at a nearby four-top. "I love it here for lunch," a woman at the table was saying. "The food's great, prices are reasonable, and you can always get a seat. You never have to wait, like at those busier places down the street."

Good for you, I thought. Not so good for me. But it was the words she spoke next that beat a giant Chinese gong in my brain. "Let's not tell anybody about this place. It'll be our secret." I vowed at that point to do whatever it took to put the Red River Grill on the map — even if it spoiled the lunch-time secret of the few regulars I had.

To get the ball rolling, I set out to determine the restaurant's strengths and weaknesses. I started at the front of the house and worked my way toward the back of the house, leaving no napkin or head of lettuce unturned. To my pleasant surprise, the place appeared to be in fine working order. Not quite as smooth as a Swiss watch, but pretty darn close.

Doubting my own point of view, I took off my business operator's hat and tried to picture the restaurant through the eyes of my guests. What did they want from the Red River Grill that it wasn't providing? Using comment cards, I sought customer feedback, only to collect a stack of mostly useless generalizations about the quality of food, service and atmosphere. Just about everything earned high marks. So how come the restaurant always had enough empty tables to handle any random bus of touring Shriners?

Feeling discouraged, I settled onto one of our barstools to collect my thoughts. On the TV anchored above, the Sports Channel was running highlights of the local basketball team's victory the night before, the same team I used to play for. There was Coach calling plays from the bench, his trademark bald head shimmering under the lights. At impact of a breakaway slam dunk, the fans in the stands erupted, cheering wildly as the Wildcats put the finishing touches on another home victory. Sipping on a double skinny latte and writing down some thoughts in a spiral notebook I always carry with me, I couldn't help but sit there thinking that one day these notes would form some secret strategy I could use to produce the same level of enthusiasm for the Red River Grill.

*— Whose dumb idea was it anyway to run an ad for the "best burgers in town" during the station's half-hour "Green Report," whose listeners are generally vegetarians and animal-rights activists?*

## CHAPTER 2
### INSIDE-OUT MARKETING

The next morning, a Monday, I jumped into my car and headed toward the Broadway Health Club. There the chronically out of shape join the hard bodies of the world in a cacophony of clanking weights and barbells, random chitchat on every imaginable subject, occasional disputed calls on the racquetball courts, and portable stereos, here and there, blasting pop music to the delight of the aerobics diehards. From my usual workout spot in the upper-level treadmill area, these diehards look like an assortment of mid-July-pickup-truck-dashboard-casualty jellybeans in their candy-colored Lycra.

To get to the club from my condominium, I can get on Broadway, the main drag through town, and head south for several miles until coming to the fountains that mark the entrance into the parking lot. Or, as I often do, I can take the scenic route through the ivy-covered university, passing the high-rise dorms I used to live in, the McCabe School of Business, the library with its stately columns and, towering above it all, the basketball arena where to this day the Wildcats remain the hottest ticket in town.

Fans, in fact, were lined up for tickets on this particular morning. Normally sold out for the season, the Wildcats had put in extra seating on the floor, behind both baskets, in preparation for the upcoming game — the biggest game of the year — against their arch rival, the Mustangs. Season ticket holders got first crack at the floor-level seats, leaving open some 100 others scattered about the arena. Yet a thousand people stood in line for a chance at seeing the game in person.

Amazing. Especially because the Wildcats, a young team this year, had already lost three games, two of them against conference opponents. No matter, the faithful and a constant stream of new fans showed up game after game, cheering on the boys whether they're winning or losing. Coach had done a remarkable job generating enthusiasm for the Wildcats, not only with his current team, but also with the teams preceding it, including the one I played on long ago. Their run-and-gun style of play and ability to rack up points in a hurry have entertained fans for years, as has the athleticism of the front-line players whose slam dunks rattle the hoop on a nightly basis.

At 6-foot-1, I could never dunk, even during my glory days, but I marveled at our players who could put it down with authority. We used to run plays, usually involving a backdoor screen, to feed the ball to a player streaking in for a dunk. Fans would go nuts over the backboard-shaking outcome, most of them never recognizing the well-coached and intricate steps executed by the *rest* of the team to set up the score in the first place.

As I sped by the arena, I daydreamed I could dunk the ball. I imagined myself taking a lane to the basket, elevating above the outstretched arms of the competition and jamming the ball two-handed over the front of the rim for the winning basket! The crowd roared in my mind as I left the school campus near the Testing Center and worked my way toward the health club.

Once inside the club, after checking in at the front desk, I ran into Coach by chance heading up the stairs leading to the treadmill machines. It's hard to miss the guy. Built like a brick tool shed with a cinder block for a head, Coach tends to stand out in a crowd. I knew he was a club member, but I rarely saw him there and figured he probably went in during odd times to avoid autograph seekers. But there he was, waiting for me at the top of the stairs. "Hey, Dean," he said, extending his right hand. "How the hell are ya?"

"Fat," I responded, shaking his hand. And to remove any doubt, I patted the extra baggage I was carrying around my waist. "Too many beers and not enough exercise — unless you count shouldering kegs and plunging clogged toilets back at the restaurant."

"I hear ya," he said, smiling. "Here to burn some of it off?"

"You got that right," I said. "On the treadmill."

"Me, too."

Coach and I took positions on adjacent treadmills and punched in the desired level of resistance and duration. We opted for the same program — level seven for 30 minutes. The machines started with a motorized whirl, sending Coach and I racing awkwardly forward as if trying to catch a bus in a rainstorm.

"How's business?" Coach finally said, after getting his second wind. An innocent question, but it unleashed many of the frustrations I had been experiencing at the Grill. The complaints rolled off my tongue faster than the wide rubber belt spinning below. *Empty tables despite the frequent-diner card I had issued months ago. Guests refusing to spread positive word of mouth about the restaurant because they want to keep the place a secret. Money going to waste on the current ad campaign on the radio. Whose dumb idea was it anyway to run an ad for the "best burgers in town" during the station's half-hour "Green Report," whose listeners are generally vegetarians and animal-rights activists?*

By this time, Coach was laughing out loud. "They're not all vegetarians and activists," he said. "Even *I* listen to the program. Your problem — if you don't mind me saying — isn't what people are *hearing* about the Red River Grill, it's what they're *getting*."

"What are you talking about?" I asked.

"It's like this," Coach said, gearing up for another one of his famous stories. "About 15, 16 years ago, just after I became head coach, we signed up this recruit out of a one-horse town deep in Texas. Ear Wax, Texas,

I think it was. This kid had a catchy nickname, 'Seven-Foot Simmons' or something like that. Our P.R. department hyped him all over the place. His sturdy frame and menacing stare appeared in media guides, press information, newspapers ... everywhere there was an audience. Before long, the town's making him out to be the greatest player on earth."

"So what happened?" I asked, unsure of what Coach was getting at, but hooked on the story nonetheless.

"Well, I'll tell ya. All the hype built up expectations — expectations the team wasn't prepared to meet. Fans thought we would finish the season undefeated. Win the National Championship. Make history. Create world peace, for crying out loud. After a while, even I started to believe it, and as a result I broke the cardinal rule of winning over fans. I over-promised what the team could accomplish and it naturally set us up to under-deliver. Which we did — big time."

"And the moral of the story is?" I still didn't get it.

"The moral is that the next season ticket sales fell off the table. Everybody — and I mean *everybody* — was bad-mouthing the program and second-guessing every decision I made. The people who hired me were now breathing down my neck. It took me a couple more seasons, not to mention a conference championship, before I finally got their confidence back."

The resistance on the treadmills increased to a steep uphill grade, forcing Coach and me to shut our traps long enough to gather the steam we needed to clear the top. Once back on level ground, we picked up the conversation where we had left off.

"The sad thing," Coach said, "was that the whole situation was avoidable. What we should have done from the beginning was take care of business inside the house — let Simmons develop at his own pace, work on team fundamentals, iron out the kinks on offense and defense, establish chemistry — long before we started blowing our own horn outside the house. Had we done that, the good press, in time, would have taken care of itself."

I nodded in agreement. The conversation, I could sense, was moving toward what was happening — or, in this case, not happening — at the Red River Grill. "If I were a gambling man," I said, "I'd bet you're going to tell me there's a lesson to be learned in the Seven Foot Simmons story."

"You're right on the money," Coach said. "But I don't think you're going to like what you hear. At least, not right now."

"Try me."

"Well, from what you've been telling me about the Grill and from what I've noticed firsthand when I've gone in for a burger, I can see your thinking's backward. You're marketing your restaurant from the outside in when you need to be approaching it from the inside out. Just like the Seven Foot Simmons fiasco. It's what you do under the roof — not what you promise on top of the roof — that counts. In our case, it's making good passes, setting up slam dunks, scoring points, playing hard-nosed defense and winning games. In your case, it's serving great food and providing the kind of service and atmosphere that makes customers line up at the door. Did you see all of our fans at the ticket booths this morning?"

"About a thousand of them," I said. "Looked like Disneyland out there."

"And that's for less than 100 tickets!" Coach said, growing more passionate by the second. Or perhaps he was just overheated by the treadmill, now picking up speed. "The key is — are you listening, Dean? — we haven't promised anything we may not be able to deliver. The Mustangs are tough this year. They could kick our butts by 50 points. But fans know, whatever the outcome, they'll see an exciting game and an honest effort out of our players."

"So are you saying the Grill hasn't done a good job of keeping its promises?" I knew the answer before Coach spoke the next words.

"That's exactly what I'm saying," he said. "You're trying to build up expectations to entice customers to try the Grill, but you're not meeting those expectations — at least not from my point of view."

Much to my chagrin, I learned that Coach had experienced the worst my restaurant had to offer, all stemming from a simple direct-mail strategy I had been executing for years. New home buyers in the area get a coupon to come into the Red River Grill and try one of our desserts for free. We were measuring redemptions, and a lot of the coupons get redeemed, so I thought I was on the right track. That is until Coach, between huffs and puffs, related what had happened to him and his wife.

"A year ago, Joan and I bought a new house — same neighborhood, but a new house," Coach began. "In the mailbox one day was a card addressed to somebody named 'Current Resident.' Didn't know the guy personally, but I did know it was from your restaurant, so I kept reading. 'Welcome to the neighborhood,' it said. 'Come on in for a free dessert.' Right away the card strikes me funny because, as you know, Dean, I've been in the neighborhood for 20 years and visiting your restaurant since it first opened."

"Kind of impersonal," I admitted, my head hung low.

"That's just the beginning," Coach continued. "At the bottom of that card, there was a group picture of your smiling servers. Underneath, it said something like: 'Our friendly staff is waiting to serve you!'"

"That's exactly what it says," I said. "Cost me one hundred dollars extra to put the picture in there."

"Probably cost you more than that," Coach said, not missing a beat. "I took that coupon to your restaurant; I think it was the same night I got it. I was going to give you a hard time, make you buy our whole dinner, not just the dessert. But I couldn't get your attention. You were busy with some operational emergency back in the kitchen."

"Probably the night the fryers went down," I said, laying the groundwork for an excuse in case I needed it.

"Fryers, earthquake, mud slide ... whatever it was, it had your attention. Which sure wasn't the case with Joan and me. We couldn't get *anyone's* attention. We sat there 20 minutes or more before a member of your quote-unquote 'friendly staff' — obviously wishing she were someplace else that night — asked if we were ready to order. 'We'll have some drinks first,' I told her, and she looked at me like I had just ruined her day. That was her attitude the rest of the meal. No friendly menu recommendations. No friendly conversation. Nothing friendly at all. We didn't even bother ordering dessert. We just left the coupon sitting right there on the table."

"I am so sorry you were treated that way," I told Coach. Shaking my head, I shifted my tongue into excuse-overdrive gear and added: "It's so hard to get good help these days. This year alone five new restaurants have opened up around us, shrinking the labor pool. There's not much we can do but hire under-qualified employees."

"Are they under-qualified or under-prepared?" Coach asked. "I mean, how hard can it be to smile and treat guests right, especially regulars? Seems to me you need to focus on getting the job done internally — through training, practice and coaching on the floor — before you waste money externally on impersonal mailers that promise things you're not ready to deliver consistently. I wonder how many other guests have come in with coupons, only to get mediocre, if not rotten, service from your staff. If I were a gambling man, I'd bet they won't be back to the Red River Grill anytime soon. In the long run, that'll cost you more than the mailer or its smiling photograph ever did."

The point had been made — painfully. As if on cue, my treadmill and then, seconds later, Coach's treadmill completed their timed cycles and came to a halt. We stood there dripping with sweat, cooling down from the workout. Coach seemed to be waiting for me to respond, but I didn't know what to say. I must have looked more disappointed than a mosquito in a wax museum because Coach, taking pity on me, spoke up.

"Don't take it so hard, Dean," he said. "The Grill does a lot of things right. Take care of a few little problems and you'll be able to reach your full potential in no time. Hey, it took me several years to win a title with the Wildcats and start attracting the big crowds. Let me tell ya — there were a lot of games when the empty seats outnumbered the filled seats 10-to-one. It got so quiet sometimes, I had to whisper to my players in the huddle so the other team couldn't hear our plays."

"That's quiet, all right," I said, feeling better. "Hopefully, it won't get *that* bad at the Grill or I'll be out of business."

"I'm sure it won't," Coach said. "I'm sure it won't."

I left the health club preoccupied with the wisdom Coach had imparted. My own Fortune 500 marketing acumen seemed paltry by comparison, my business degree all of a sudden not worth the paper it was written on. I had invested heavily in external marketing strategies of all kinds, but compromised their potential to make a profit and generate repeat business by not investing an equal, if not greater, amount on my *internal* marketing. In other words, I had neglected to make sure the Grill's quality of service matched the expectations raised in its marketing materials. Hard-earned money down the drain.

As I drove home, following in reverse the same route I took to the club, I thought about the promises I had made to customers during the past year. "Best burgers in town." "Where the action is." "Friendly service." "Not your usual neighborhood restaurant."

Truth is, however, we were usual — usually mediocre from a customer-service standpoint. No better than the dry cleaner who lures your business with a 2-for-1 shirt offer but then, calling your attention to the small print on the back of your receipt, won't fix the button it broke on your best suit. No better than the car wash whose change machine has ripped you off once again while advertising "10 minutes for only a quarter." No better than the coffee shop which, even after years of everyday patronage, can't remember if you take whole or skim milk in your latte.

It was overwhelming to think of all that needed to be done to market the Red River Grill from the inside out. The predicament made me think of a game, an important conference game, I once played in. Down by 20 points with less than five minutes left to play, we were casting off shots right and left, trying to close the gap. Coach called timeout to quell the panic. He said: "There's only one way to eat an elephant, gentlemen. One bite at a time." And that's what we did. We whittled down the lead basket by basket, then won the game on a well-orchestrated, alley-oop slam dunk — just in time to beat the buzzer.

One bite at a time — that's how I'd shore up the internal marketing at my restaurant, paying less attention to the advertisements placed by my competitors and more attention to the service provided by my staff. I'd collect every one of our ads, coupons and radio scripts — past or present — and make a list of all the statements raising customer expectations. I didn't know how yet, but I'd train our servers, bartenders and greeters to exceed those expectations. I'd personally coach "our team" to set up and execute its own slam dunks. We'd create both winners and word-of-mouth excitement to get "new fans." At the very least, I'd keep our promises.

At each of the stoplights on the way home, I wrote down a few reminders in what I now was calling my marketing notebook.

Seven Foot Simmons
External vs. Internal
Great Expectations
No Train? No Gain!
Up Close and Personal

By the time I reached the basketball arena, the roar of the crowd I had imagined in the morning was replaced with a hollow silence, a mix of worry and contemplation, that distracted me the rest of the day. I went to bed early that night, exhausted but too restless to sleep peacefully. I had a nightmare about the Grill. I saw crickets, with coal-black eyes and nervous tentacles, chirping inside the vacant restaurant. Cobwebs stretching from the ceilings to the floors. Incredible wads of petrified gum sticking under seats and barstools. A CLOSED sign hanging in the window.

Outside the front door was an old bum, clad in dirty, moth-eaten clothes and wing-tip shoes that had seen better days. He was shaking nickels and dimes collected in an old soup can, begging passers-by for spare change. For the longest time, I couldn't see who the man was. Then finally his toothless, unshaven face turned into view. At that instant, I woke up chilled and short of breath, but greatly relieved to find all my teeth still intact.

What I didn't realize, however, was that the nightmare had just begun.

— *"Did you do that shaving or did you
try to kiss a cat?"* *he asked.*

# CHAPTER 3
## THE STAR TREATMENT

Come morning I shaved twice, making sure the person in the mirror resembled as little as possible the pallid, whiskered face unveiled in the nightmare I had just awakened from. I'm not one to try to decipher the meaning of dreams — most of the time I can't even remember what I've dreamed — but this one hung with me like an onion sandwich. The second time around with the razor, in fact, I was too distracted to concentrate and nicked my face up one side and down the other, drawing blood from numerous spots.

I stopped the bleeding with bits and pieces of tissue paper, which, in my troubled state, I forgot to remove before entering the Red River Grill at 10:30 a.m., about an hour and a half later than I usually arrive for work. It was Tuesday. The front-of-the-house staff was preparing for the lunch shift, setting up tables and booths, filling ketchup bottles, stacking roll-ups in the bin next to the clean glasses, combing hair and donning uniforms — among other chores. In the back of the house, the cooks were prepping onions, tomatoes, lettuce, pepperoni, grilled chicken and sausage, five types of cheese and other items destined for the menu offerings, primarily burgers, salads and mini-pizzas, which we'd sell that shift.

The first person I ran into was Kate, my general manager, who wasted no time going for the jugular. "You look like scary papier maché art," she said.

"Thanks a lot," I responded, remembering the first aid I had applied. "I'll be right back." I went into the bathroom to peel away the tissue without aggravating the wounds. I did look pretty scary. And if that weren't enough, I was having a bad hair day.

Upon my return from the bathroom, Kate was opening the front doors for another day of business. We met up at a corner booth to go over several matters. I was anxious to tell her about the conversation I'd had with Coach the day before on the treadmill machines. But first things first. She wanted to review applications for a server opening and, as I vaguely recall, discuss some upgrades we were considering for the beer-dispensing system. My mind, however, was drifting off above the clouds.

"Dean to planet earth," Kate said, then increased the volume. *"Dean to planet earth!"*

"Let's, uh, go for the, um, Empty Beer Detector Valves," I sputtered, pretending I had been following the conversation all along.

It was no use. Kate was on to me. "You haven't heard a word I've said."

28

"No, I guess I haven't. It's just that, number one, I had a nightmare last night that's been giving me the jitters."

"What was it about?" Kate asked.

"The restaurant — or what was left of it. In my dream, it was boarded up, out of business for no apparent reason. There were cobwebs everywhere ... crickets ... and, out front, an old bum that turned out to be me begging for change. Scared the hell out of me."

"What's the deal? Did you have a bad taco before you went to bed?" Kate wasn't taking the ordeal as seriously as I was.

"No, I think it came from what Coach and I talked about at the health club. He told me some things that really got me thinking."

"About what?" Kate said, more interested now.

"About the way we market the restaurant — from the outside in rather than from the inside out, which is what we should be doing."

I related the story about Coach and his wife visiting the Grill to redeem the dessert coupon they received after moving into their new home. I mentioned the poor service they had encountered, which started when they were sent our direct-mail piece addressed to "Current Resident" and ended with one of our servers totally neglecting their needs. The story, I told Kate, underscored the importance of making sure we have our act together *internally* before we spend money on external-marketing schemes to build traffic.

"Under-promise and over-deliver," I said, using my thumb and forefinger to count the points. "It's been said many times before, but that's the key. And, too much of the time, I think we're doing just the opposite."

"I don't know what to say," Kate said. Her normally upbeat expression melted like an ice cream cone on the Fourth of July.

At that moment, the first guests of the day — two couples, both probably married — entered through the foyer and approached an empty hostess stand. Kelly, our hostess that shift, was nowhere in sight. Jessie, usually our best server, walked by the guests and, not saying a word, disappeared down the stairs heading toward the bathrooms. Other servers appeared equally preoccupied. Apparently, we were running behind. I could tell the people waiting were starting to wonder if the place was open. I had to step in and seat them.

"Your server will be right with you," I said, handing each guest a menu. But I wasn't entirely sure that would indeed be the case.

It was starting to get busy, and Kate and I sped around the restaurant to jump-start the sluggish crew. When the show was finally up and running, I selected a pivot point from which to keep an eye on things. As more and more lunch guests filed in, I noticed something peculiar. I didn't know any of them. Not one. You'd think, after six and a half years of running the Red River Grill, I'd recognize a professor from the university or an employee of the ShopSmart down the street or one of the mechanics that change oil at the nearby Speedy Lube. Don't get me wrong, regulars did come in from time to time, but on this day, for all I knew, everybody in the place was a newcomer.

It occurred to me — of course, now it seems painfully obvious — that we weren't doing nearly enough to get customers to come back and bring along their friends. There was no concrete plan to turn newcomers into regulars. I began to think that I had overestimated the power of good food alone to do the trick. One by one, I stared at the strangers seated at the tables, wondering what was going through their minds. My gaze settled on the power lunch of two businessmen, Mr. Purple Tie and Mr. Mustache, who were eating our Chopped Salad and splitting a Five-Cheese Pizza. What was it that brought them in that day? What would it take to secure their business once or twice a week? I had no clue.

At the end of the lunch rush — if you could call it a rush — I decided I had the time to rectify my bad-hair situation. I didn't have an appointment, but I knew Lou, owner of the Downtown Barbershop, would work me into his schedule. After all, I'd been getting my ears lowered there for years, dating back to my basketball-playing days. A lot of the Wildcat players, past and present, frequent the barbershop, as do university and sports officials and a huge number of fans. It's considered good luck, especially before important games.

Inside the Downtown Barbershop, photographs of current players and all-time greats, mixed in with photos of regular customers, adorn the Wall of Fame opposite the big mirror in which Lou works his magic. At the base of the mirror, running its full length, is a counter topped with stacks of *Sports Illustrated*, an ancient AM radio tuned into *SportsTalk*, a dish filled with peppermint candy, and assorted tools of the barber's trade, including a straight-edge razor Lou sharpens, when needed, on a leather strap attached to the swiveling chair.

After a short wait, I took my turn in the seat of honor. Lou immediately noticed all the cuts on my face. "Did you do that shaving or did you try to kiss a cat?" he asked.

"Not enough shaving cream, I guess."

"I don't think plaster of Paris would have saved you from those gashes," Lou said. "Tell you what — next time you come in, I'll give you the best shave of your life. On me."

"You got a deal," I said.

By this time, Lou had sprayed down my hair with water and was beginning to take an inch off the top. I didn't have to tell him what I wanted; he already knew. To this day, Lou has the uncanny ability to remember not only the names of his regulars, but also the myriad ways they like their hair done — including seasonal variances. I'm talking hundreds and hundreds of customers. I had taken this skill of his for granted until, in the time it took to turn me into a young Marlon Brando wannabe, I began to see the internal-marketing applications for my own business.

Most impressive was the fact that Lou welcomed, by name, every regular that entered the door. He even recognized *half* the people that just walked by on the outside. More than one paused at the window, next to the red-and-white spiraling barber pole, to get Lou's attention and mouth the words telling when they'd be in next. Lou read their lips and, with a wave of his scissors hand, confirmed the day and time.

Lou was raking the back of my neck with an electric razor when some guy he *didn't* know came into the shop. Lou wasted no time. "Need a haircut?" he began.

"Sure do," the man said. "Can you take me today?"

"I've got an opening at four o'clock."

"That'll work fine."

"Your name?"

"Robert Henneman."

"Well, Robert, I'll see you then at four. Or come earlier if you want. The new S.I. is in."

And just like that, Lou added another name to his list. You can bet that Robert would be greeted personally every time he patronized the shop, which would probably be once a month. Why go anywhere else? People want to go where everyone knows their name. At $15 a haircut, plus, on average, a $2 tip, Robert represented $204 in annual revenue for the Downtown Barbershop. Multiply that by an ever-growing number of regulars, and it was easy to see how Lou's personal slam dunks helped pay for the expensive sports car parked out front.

Lou doesn't offer the cheapest haircut in town — far from it — but what he does offer is an *experience* that more than justifies the added expense. Part of his marketing game plan is to offer "$5 off your next haircut" coupons to the basketball players, many of whom aren't on scholarship and don't have much money to spare. They're often in the barbershop talking hoops with the gossip-starved customers and feeding the sports atmosphere of the place. Now that's a slam-dunk approach, if I ever saw one.

Contemplating the allure of the Downtown Barbershop got me thinking about the conveniences that increase the frequency of my own visits. First of all, Lou is always willing to squeeze me in — appointment or no appointment. That counts big in my book because my workdays are so unstructured. On this occasion, he offered me a free shave on my next visit, which I would gladly take him up on. On the Wall of Fame, there's a black-and-white photograph of me dishing a no-look pass to a player, far more famous than me, driving in for a score. Sometimes I get a haircut just to shoot the bull and reminisce about the old days. Lou always points out that picture to other customers and makes me out to be something special in the history of the Wildcats program. Truth is, I was pretty mediocre as a basketball player, but Lou makes me feel like a star.

Every six weeks, right on the dot, customers receive a postcard reminding them it's time for a haircut. Lou built the mailing list by placing a fishbowl on a stand near the exit and asking patrons to drop in a business card for a chance to win a free haircut. If you don't have a business card, no problem. You can fill out one of the forms stacked nearby.

"When do you have time to enter all those names and addresses into a computer?" I once asked Lou.

"Don't have to enter them," he said. "I got me a scanner and software that can read the business cards and the forms. Just feed them in and the information goes right into the database file — in alphabetical order."

It dawned on me that day that Lou was far more sophisticated than his old-fashioned barbershop would suggest. For effect, he used antique tools of the barber's trade. For profit, he merchandised a leading brand-name line of hair products and used technology to increase the frequency of customer visits. Of course, high tech took a back seat to high touch.

At Lou's, everyone, whether you're in the chair or waiting in the wings, gets drawn in by name to the topic of discussion. The wait goes quickly, especially if you're a Wildcat fan, because Lou collects all the popular sports magazines and plays *SportsTalk* radio all day long. Matter of fact, he's occasionally quoted in the sports page of the daily newspaper, the reporters seeking his historical perspective.

No one — except for Coach — has been around the basketball program longer than Lou. He attends virtually every game and advertises in the back of the programs.

The ads themselves are great. They show Coach, with his patented bald head, sitting in Lou's barber chair. Underneath it says: "Best Haircut in Town!"

Believe it or not, I even appreciate the mints Lou gives away. I always take a few with me to ward off the consequences of sampling too much garlic bread at the restaurant. The conclusion of this day's haircut was no different. I left a twenty-dollar bill on the counter, sized up the "new me" in the mirror and picked up a handful of candy on the way out.

"Thanks, Dean, I really appreciate your business," Lou said. "I'll see you in about a month. And don't forget about that free shave. You should be healed up by then."

"Yeah, unless gangrene sets in," I said.

Unknowingly, Lou had taught me a valuable lesson in generating repeat business. It's not necessarily any one big thing you do, it's a combination of the little things that add up to success. As I hopped into my car and headed back to work, I couldn't help but feel a couple steps closer to where I wanted the Red River Grill to be. First Coach had altered my marketing mindset, then Lou had filled in some of the gaps.

Internal marketing ideas sprang to mind faster than a jackalope with its tail on fire. I'd have a heart-to-heart with the front-of-the-house staff about customer service, telling everybody, without naming names, what had happened the time Coach came in with his wife. I'd work on learning and using guests' names. I'd figure

© Pencom International • 800-247-8514

out a way to use pictures of customers to make them feel like stars — the same way *I* always feel at Lou's. I'd keep around some current magazines and newspapers for guests, especially solo diners, to read and pass the time. I'd look for ways to capitalize on my connections with the Wildcats basketball program. I'd go out of my way to thank people for their business.

My creative marketing juices were overflowing by the time I reached the restaurant. Before I had a chance to forget anything, I used my secret shorthand to record the ideas in my marketing notebook.

The first thing I wanted to do was put an end to the dessert coupons we'd been sending to "Current Residents." Instead, I'd work up a more personal approach involving free T-shirts and discounts on beer and spirits during happy hour. Something along the lines of Lou's "$5 off" coupons and drawings for a free haircut. So pleased was I with my newfound genius that I didn't realize it was the dumbest thing I could have decided to do.

Heart to Heart
Skip to the Lou
Point and Shoot
The Star Treatment
Something Special
Gone Fishing
GO WILDCATS!

— *"To be successful and make every penny count,
I have to generate what I call
'One-Two' Customer Traffic."*

# CHAPTER 4
## "ONE-TWO" TRAFFIC

By Friday afternoon the details were nearly worked out on the marketing strategy Lou had unknowingly inspired from his post in the Downtown Barbershop. Kate and I, working long hours together for days, decided to revamp what had been a so-so happy hour at the Red River Grill. We had never made the event a top priority, which in retrospect was a mistake. Why do something if you're not going to give it your best shot?

Our new-and-improved happy hour, scheduled to take place from 4:30 to 5:30 p.m. each night of the week, would feature a "Buy One, Get One Free" special on draft beer and an "Extra Shot for Only a $1 More" discount on mixed drinks. We figured we could not only attract new business through the doors, but also reward the regulars who congregated around the bar after work.

During the first week of the promotion, we planned to set up a fishbowl by the greeter stand to collect business cards for nightly drawings. We'd give away T-shirts bearing the Red River Grill logo on the back. A local silk-screener gave us a volume discount — $8 apiece — for an order of 250. The information gleaned from the business cards would be input into a database, enabling us to address future mailings to *real* people rather than "Current Residents."

Taking another cue from Lou, we'd make an effort to learn and use the names of guests, especially first-timers, making everyone feel welcome and appreciated. To start our own Wall of Fame, we bought a point-and-shoot camera to take pictures of people smiling and enjoying themselves. Perhaps Coach would even drop by one night for a mug shot, which I'd be sure to hang in a place of honor. We'd advertise the details of the promotion on a banner hung in the front window of the restaurant and on table tents placed on every table-top and in front of every other barstool. If the initial response to the new happy hour was encouraging, we'd also run ads in the programs at Wildcat games.

On paper, the event looked like a winner. The banner and table tents would be ready in a week. If all went well, we'd get the $275 investment back along with the extra margins we'd generate in only three days! Prior to opening night, we'd brief the front of the house on the happy hour, going over the details and what we wanted the staff to do. Kate and I were giddy with excitement. So giddy, in fact, that Kate decided to take the weekend off and I made plans to attend the basketball game that night.

Lacking the time for most leisure activities, I had gotten in the habit of giving my ticket away on game nights, usually to one of my employees. But I kept it this time, not wanting to miss the long-awaited showdown between the Mustangs and Wildcats. The game, of course, was the talk of the town. You couldn't walk into any public place, from the gas station to the grocery store, without hearing opinions about who'd win and why.

The local TV stations had been running team features every night of the week preceding the tip-off, including what I considered to be blatant advertising — a report alerting fans that the first 1,000 in the arena would receive an authentic Wildcat towel commemorating the big game. It would be a sure collector's item and just the thing to spin overhead like a lasso to distract opposing players on the free-throw line. The news anchors treated the story with all the seriousness of a political coup.

Towels would be just part of the picture. In all Wildcat games, fans in attendance can come away with team Frisbees which the cheerleaders let fly into the stands during breaks in the action. At half time, randomly selected ticket holders get to try hard-to-make shots at the hoop for a chance to win prizes. The tougher the shot, the better the prize — all put up by the arena's corporate sponsors. There's even a miniature blimp, remotely controlled, that cruises around the rafters dropping "You Win!" tokens into the outstretched hands of enthusiastic fans. The tokens can be redeemed for any number of team souvenirs.

The concession stands, far too many to count, move mind-boggling amounts of hot dogs, cotton candy, nachos, red-licorice ropes and other artery-clogging products. And to wash it all down, there's an endless supply of beer and soft drinks. The whole Wildcat-watching experience is a marketing masterpiece.

That's what I was thinking to myself as I handed my ticket to the attendant at the door a few minutes prior to game time. Before reaching Portal A, the one leading to my seat, I bumped into Lucinda Robertson, a close friend of mine who manages sales and marketing at the arena. She was straightening a row of stuffed animals — Wildcats, of course — at one of the souvenir stands.

"Dean, how are you? Seems like I haven't seen you forever," Lucinda said, still going about her work.

"I've been swamped," I said. "Looks like you have your hands full, too."

"You have no idea. Getting everything done in time for this game has made me busier than a one-armed wallpaper hanger with insomnia." Lucinda stepped back from the display to check her alignment. "But now, I'm happy to say, my work is done."

"You deserve a raise," I said.

"Because I can put stuffed animals in a straight line?"

"No, because this place rakes it in game after game," I said.

The roar of the crowd interrupted our conversation. The game had begun and, from the sound of it, the Wildcats had scored the first basket.

"Where you sitting?" Lucinda asked.

"Center court, 20 rows up."

"Tell you what," she said. "Ever watched the game from the sky box?"

"I've been in there, but never to watch a game."

"Let's go. We can catch up on life."

Lucinda and I took back seats in the sky box, leaving room up front for a seemingly mismatched group of V.I.P. sponsors who had provided lavish prizes in exchange for halftime exposure, executives from the school's novelty store and an assistant coach who was taping the game. Down on the court, the Wildcats, 10-point underdogs, were building a comfortable lead.

"So, how are things at the Red River Grill?" Lucinda began.

"Can't complain, really," I said. "But I'd be a whole lot better off if I were just half the marketer you are."

"Oh, I don't know about that," she said. "I think you're giving me too much credit. In my mind, marketing isn't as complicated as a lot of people make it out to be. A little creativity, a little common sense — that's half of it right there."

"I think you're oversimplifying a bit," I said. Several of my own sub-par marketing ventures sprang to mind.

"Maybe, but I don't think so," Lucinda said. "The mistake I see people make again and again is that they view a particular promotion as an end in itself. What they don't realize is that effective marketing isn't a one-shot deal. Let me give you an example. We gave away 1,000 towels tonight — nice ones, too. They cost us five bucks each to produce. Why do we do that?"

"Why *do* you do that?" I asked. "Especially when you know ahead of time the game's a sellout."

"Fans love the towels is the easy answer," Lucinda continued. "But we also get a lot of marketing mileage out of them. Was it worth five bucks a towel to get every news station in town to cover the promotion? You bet. We've also found that fans who get something cool for free are more likely to go all out at the concession stands. The value added to their experience may even prompt them to buy additional merchandise. At the very least, it further secures their team loyalty, which is good for ticket sales down the road."

"You thought of all those things when coming up with the towel-giveaway idea?" I asked.

"That's my job. Believe it or not, my marketing budget is tight. To be successful and make every penny count, I have to generate what I call 'One-Two' Customer Traffic."

"One-Two?" I asked.

"Like a one-two combination of punches in boxing," Lucinda explained. "In other words, it's not enough to get people in the door. Anybody can do that.

The trick, at least in our business and probably yours, is to sell those people something while they're there. And do it in a way that enhances their experience so they come back for more. Repeat business is the name of the game."

One look around the arena confirmed her point. Fans upon fans were munching on food, guzzling beverages, wearing team ballcaps, jerseys and warm-up jackets, poring over $5 game programs, cheering on the basketball team — all in all having the time of their lives.

"Tickets account for only part, a small part, of the overall dollars generated at a game," Lucinda said. "Without multiple sources of revenue, the Wildcats would be playing in a barn, and I'd be hawking bargain jewelry on the Shopping Channel."

"Or handling the marketing for a beer-and-burger joint like mine," I said.

"Not even *I* would stoop *that* low," she said with a laugh. Soon after that remark, the buzzer sounded, signaling the end of the first half. Lucinda had to run down to the floor to oversee the festivities. On this night they were prepared to award a trip to the Bahamas if some lucky fan could sink a three-point shot. Fat chance, I thought, as the nervous contestant reached mid-court and proceeded to bounce the ball off his foot.

The Wildcats were up by eight points at the half, plenty of reason to be excited and into the game, but I found myself taking out the notebook again from my back pocket. I jotted down the words "One-Two Traffic" and, underneath the phrase, a reminder of what it meant. Trepidation began to replace the confidence I had felt early on in developing the happy hour improvements. But for some reason I couldn't bring myself to postpone the plans Kate and I had made.

I sat there watching the second half of the game, barely aware the Wildcats were pulling off the upset victory. I was too busy rationalizing why — ready or not — we should go forward with the new promotion. *It's only a simple happy hour after all. It's better than the last version we had. We can fine-tune as we go. Enough stalling already!*

The happy hour ideas Kate and I had come up with weren't poorly conceived. It's just that, despite our best intentions, our efforts were destined to come up short for reasons that became more clear as time passed.

After we rolled out the happy hour on schedule, business picked up as expected, but it created a false sense of security. We'd learn the hard way that increasing traffic by decreasing margins can produce lackluster results, especially when you don't maximize add-on sales during the promotion or do what's necessary to generate repeat customers willing to pay full price on a future visit.

We went into the first night of the promotion thinking the dollars would take care of themselves. It didn't quite happen that way. We made three big mistakes, and probably lots of little ones.

*Mistake number one:* The bottom line. We failed to determine a sales strategy to compensate for the profit margins we'd narrowed on the "Buy One, Get One Free" beers and the extra shots for a dollar. Lucinda had talked at length about the importance of generating One-Two Traffic, and I understood what she had said. But there's a difference between knowing what to do and getting it done. Bottom line, we didn't train our employees to suggest appetizers to go along with the beverage orders or upgrade cocktail orders to include premium spirits. Considering all the costs associated with the event, our return on investment left much to be desired. Too many guests took advantage of the happy hour, only to take off at the end having not ordered any food.

*Mistake number two:* The T-shirts. First of all, they were of high quality and cost us a bundle to produce. Guests were happy to receive one in the nightly drawings, and they might even wear it around town, giving the Grill some free advertising. But it dawned on us later that it's probably best to put the logo on the front, where it's more readily noticed. What's more, the T-shirts by themselves lacked the pull to encourage a high percentage of return visits to our restaurant. We should have made wearing them part of an ongoing promotion: "Wear the T-shirt and receive a free appetizer with the purchase of an entree the *next* time you come in and every Friday during basketball season." Or something like that.

In other words, establish a bounceback offer. Clearly, more brainstorming needed to be done.

*Mistake number three:* The fishbowl. What started as a simple idea turned into a nightmare. We hired an hourly employee, at minimum wage, to input the business-card information into a computer file that could be merged with any number of marketing pieces we developed. As the first step — and as sort of a test — we sent thank-you notes to the first week of guests who put their cards into the fishbowl. Problem was, some people didn't have cards so they wrote on the back of someone else's, but invariably didn't put down enough information. A lot of other people threw in more than one card, and we forgot to check for duplicate names on the 332 mailings that went out. Our employee actually noticed the problem but, drawing on a supernatural IQ, he figured it was supposed to be that way. The Red River Grill has never been more generous with its graciousness. Hell, one of our regulars got thanked 10 times. The screwup not only embarrassed us, but also drove up the happy hour expenses all the more.

About the time we came to these disappointing conclusions, Lucinda dropped by the restaurant for a visit. The night we had sat together at the big game, a problem had arisen at half time, preventing her return to the sky box. She came to apologize and eat a bite of lunch. I joined her at the table, both of us splitting a quesadilla appetizer and a Grilled Chicken Caesar.

"Sorry about that night last week," Lucinda said, between bites. "We had run out of Wildcat basketballs — kids just go nuts over them — and I was looking for an extra box I knew I had tucked away somewhere. I searched the rest of the night, but I couldn't find it. Still haven't found it."

"No need to apologize," I said. "It was actually productive to sit there alone absorbing the marketing advice you'd given me."

"Did it help?"

"Well, to be honest ..."

"Uh-oh, I'm sensing trouble," Lucinda interrupted.

"It was nothing that you said," I continued. "In fact, what you said about generating One-Two Traffic was a real eye-opener for me. We tried to incorporate it into a new happy hour promotion we had in the works, but in the end we just didn't execute very well."

"Happens to the best of us," Lucinda consoled. "I remember this one halftime promotion. We pulled six fans out of the stands and had them put an umbrella between their forehead and the floor. We made them spin around and around — something like 10 times — then had them try to make a layup. What a disaster! Two guys stumbled head first into each other, knocking both out cold. A third person, a woman, got nauseated and threw up on the court. The other participants were too dizzy to put the ball in the basket before time ran out, so we ended up with three injuries and no winners."

"Holy cow!" I felt better already about our shortcomings with the happy hour.

Lucinda wasn't through. "I had no idea, Dean, that you planned to take what I said about marketing and put it to use overnight. Otherwise I'd have stressed the importance of planning and execution. More often than not, you can't just pull the trigger on some idea you've dreamed up. You have to think it out, develop a game plan, execute and follow up, analyzing what worked and what didn't work."

"You're sounding a lot like a coach," I said.

"Well, think about it," Lucinda went on. "It's exactly like Coach and his Wildcats. Long before they work on slam dunking the basketball, they fine-tune their offense — their plan of attack — which sets up the possibility of a slam dunk in the first place. Without a game plan, the Wildcats wouldn't have won the other night. *With* a game plan, they were able to knock off probably the best team in the league."

Lucinda was right. It's better to execute a mediocre idea properly than botch a promising idea, which is what happened with our happy hour. Not all was lost, however. Repairs were under way to fix the damage caused by the duplicate mailings. We also invested in two off-the-shelf training videos — one covering the art of suggesting and selling craft beer, the other demonstrating upselling techniques with appetizers. Both promised to teach our servers how to improve service while building check averages. We showed five-minute segments of each video at our daily team meetings. We quit giving away T-shirts. Slowly but surely, we were shoring up our marketing approach.

As we ate, I reviewed and added to the reminders in my marketing notebook.

After Lucinda finished her lunch and was headed out the door, she turned and said: "We've been talking a lot about short-term marketing measures, but you know there's a long-term angle, too. You hear what I'm saying, Dean?"

No End in Sight

One-Two Traffic

Add It On

DEAN RULES   Polite, Not Pushy

Training Revisited

Bouncebacks

Fix the Fish

I heard what she was saying all right. What she meant, however, was a whole different story.

— *".... the most effective approach is personal, whether it's on the phone, face to face or in writing. The key word is personal."*

## CHAPTER 5
### THE SHORT AND LONG OF IT

After Lucinda walked out the door, my head was spinning about what to do with the Red River Grill. After tending to some new inventory posting business, I ended up where I always end up in times of contemplation — on the last stool at the end of the bar nursing a double skinny latte and going over the entries in my newly christened "official marketing notebook."

Over the past couple of weeks, I'd run into several friends and acquaintances who, consciously or unconsciously, had shared with me their marketing insights. Valuable ones, too, shedding light on internal versus external marketing, turning newcomers into regulars and generating One-Two Traffic. At this point in acquiring the *Slam Dunk Marketing* principles, however, I could see that I was long on ideas but short on how and when to execute them.

I considered what Lucinda had said before she left — something about a long-term angle to my short-term marketing measures. As I tried to make sense of the comment, Sid, our head bartender, tuned in the TV to Coach's Corner, a widely watched program in which Coach recaps highlights of the previous game and invites players to talk about their contributions to a victory or efforts to stave off a defeat. This particular show was filled with smiles and adulation, the Wildcats still celebrating the big win over the Mustangs.

Toward the end of the broadcast, the show's host asked Coach to predict how his team would fare the rest of the year. Coach was too smart to make promises he couldn't keep. "It's a long season," he said. "We're just focused on winning one game at a time."

Ah, yes. The tried-and-true "We'll win 'em one at a time" response. Coach had used it for years, leaving the prognosticating to the local prognosticators. But as I heard the words this time, they took on new meaning for me. It is indeed a long season for any business, especially the casual-theme restaurant business. The Grill, more than ever before, needed a win in the marketing column. A sure thing. A slam dunk.

Before I rushed into anything — an all-too-common mistake for me lately — I'd take whatever steps I could to ensure success. And I'd start by sending flowers to Lucinda, not only to thank her for taking an interest in my marketing efforts, but also to express my own interest in going out with her. I was growing more and more fond of her company.

Within walking distance of the restaurant is Mother Earth Flowers, owned and operated by Mother Earth herself, Franny Copeland. You usually see her wearing a floral sun dress, even in the dead of winter, and a floppy straw hat decorated with white-silk lilies. She'd come across as a grandmotherly type if it weren't for the "Flower Power" tattoo on her right bicep. Franny recognized me immediately as I entered the shop's front door.

"Dean!" she said at the top of her lungs. "The best restaurateur in town and my best customer." The other customers in the place gave me a quick glance, then went about their business.

"What'll it be today?" Franny asked. "Roses for Kate after working all that overtime at the Grill? No, don't tell me. An arrangement for your mother. Hey, we could do something nice with some scarborough and crabtree."

"What are you trying to say, Franny?" I asked. "That my mom's a crab?"

"You're the one that brought it up. Didn't you tell me the other day that she cussed out the delivery boy for not double-wrapping the rubberband around her newspaper?"

"She didn't want any of the CD-ROM coupons to fall out," I said, trying to defend mom's actions. "She collects them."

Franny couldn't resist needling me further. "What was it she called the kid — a butt-head?"

"She's been watching too much MTV," I countered. "Anyway, she's not the one I'm buying the flowers for."

I went on to place an order for a dozen roses, including a card that took me 15 minutes or more to write. I chose the words carefully, trying to hint at my feelings for Lucinda without being too forward. "Thanks for all your help," the note began. "I appreciate your expertise almost as much as your friendship."

Franny completed my order, which, according to the Mother Earth's "Dozen Dozen" punch card I kept in my wallet, was the 11th time I had sent a dozen roses since this frequent-buyer promotion began. After the 12th punch, my next purchase of a dozen would be free.

I felt good about the value punching the card added to my purchase — long stems, after all, cost an arm and a leg — and I was surprised to find myself wondering who I'd send that free arrangement to. I realized that the promotion had not only helped secure my loyalty as a customer for more than a year, but also increased the frequency of my visits.

Punch cards are nothing new, but what impressed me about Franny's was her zealousness in keeping on top of the details. The card itself was smartly designed. Instead of a normal punch, she used one that made holes in the shape of a rose. Every new customer who came in the door heard a pitch for the promotion, reinforced by posters hanging on the wall and a call to action printed on every sales receipt: "Get your Dozen Dozen Card today." And a month before every traditional flower-buying holiday, card-carrying customers received a call or message on their telephone answering machines from Mother Earth reminding them to place their upcoming orders early and to bring in their cards.

It takes a long time to send a "Dozen Dozen," so Franny constantly reminded regulars to put their cards someplace where they wouldn't lose them. Or if they wanted, she'd keep them on file, in alphabetical order, next to the cash register. On more than one occasion, I watched her give a V.I.P. customer an extra punch with a wink of an eye. In fact, I saw it happen to Coach, who made a habit of sending roses to the wives of his assistant coaches — his way of apologizing for all the long hours he kept their husbands away from home.

Now it was my turn for Franny's generosity. "Let me see your Dozen Dozen Card," she said. At which point she punched out the two remaining spots. "Next dozen's on me." Then she filled out a new card and handed it to me.

"You didn't have to do that," I said. "But I'm glad you did."

"Least I could do for my best customer."

"Tell me, Franny, how's this promotion been working out for you? I'm in the middle of overhauling my own marketing at the Red River Grill, and I'm always on the lookout for ideas." I was just making conversation, but I'd also learned that you never know when you're going to pick up a few pointers.

"The promotion's going well — really well," she said. "Better than my competitors probably think."

"What do you mean?" I asked.

"Well, in the customer's mind, the Dozen Dozen Card holds a $39 value, the average price of 12 long-stem roses. I'm not sure too many florists are willing to give that much away or commit to a long-term promotion of this kind. They're after short-term results. Usually a one-day traffic-builder — Mother's Day or Valentine's Day, for example — then it's back to business as usual. I do those, too, but I don't place too much stock in a string of quick fixes. I'm more interested in the long run, not overly preoccupied with chasing new customers but maximizing my service and profit potential with the customers I already have."

"You don't want new customers?" I asked. I wasn't following Franny's logic.

"Of course, I want new customers," she said. "Who doesn't? But I can tell you that it's far more cost effective to market to people who are already familiar with your products and services than to persuade strangers to give you a try. For me, it all comes down to picking and choosing the short-term marketing opportunities that will enable you to reach your long-term goals. What's more, I've found that most of the new cards we issue come about because of referrals from our satisfied regulars, so they're doing our marketing to strangers for us."

"Tell me more," I said. I recalled that Lucinda had also mentioned the long-term angle. Perhaps Franny, this tattooed Mother Earth, was about to connect the dots for me.

"All right, Dean. You tell me something first. I want to hear about one of your more successful promotions."

It took me a minute or two to come up with one, but I described the "Winning Streak" promotion Kate and I had run a couple of years back. The Wildcats were on a tear at that time, eventually winning 16 games in a row. Eight games into the streak, we'd worked up a marketing strategy involving our popular Cajun Shrimp Basket, which usually contains eight pieces for $6.95. For the same price, we vowed to add a shrimp to the basket for every consecutive Wildcats victory. We didn't even have to advertise the event. The media outlets caught wind of it, and their reports sent tons of business our way. The Cajun spices also worked up everyone's thirst, increasing beverage sales enough to cover the growing food cost on the dish and leave us with a nice return on investment. We were thrilled with the results.

"Great idea!" Franny spouted when I was finished. "So what happened?"

"The Wildcats finally lost, and we went back to the old Shrimp Basket."

"And all those customers new to your restaurant who gorged themselves on Cajun Shrimp — what happened to them?"

"I'm not sure," I said. "My guess would be that some came back for another visit and others didn't."

"And what about your regulars who took part in the promotion — did they respond to your restaurant any differently than they had before?"

"I have no idea," I said.

"You've illustrated my point exactly," Franny said. "You were pleased with your short-term results, but you failed to integrate a long-term component into your marketing strategy. That's what I mean by maximizing your service and profit potential with the customers you've worked so hard to get in the doors. You had 'em — thanks to an effective short-term approach — then you let 'em go, perhaps without a reason to return. You'll never know for sure because you didn't set something up for the long run."

Coach, Lou the barber, Lucinda and now Franny. I was beginning to suspect that my friends thought of me as an idiot. I wasn't ready to don any dunce cap just yet.

"OK, you got me. What could I have done long-term-wise?" I asked Franny.

"Oh, I don't know," she said. "I obviously haven't given it much thought. But the easiest would have been to meet them personally, learn their names and use that one-on-one charm you and Kate are so good at. If you learn one thing about marketing, Dean, remember that the most effective approach is personal, whether it's on the phone, face to face or in writing. The key word is *personal*."

Franny had more to say. "And if you wanted to get fancy, you could have tried, say, a tie-in with ticket holders. While they were eating their shrimp, you could have had them write their names, addresses and phone numbers on ticket stubs, which then go into the hopper for prize drawings during the winning streak. The customer information you gathered could have formed the foundation for a targeted mailing to generate repeat business down the road. Who knows? You might have been able to capitalize on the Wildcats' recent win by using that database for a telephone campaign to build your business after the game. The same thing I do when I call you or leave a message on your answering machine."

"Never crossed my mind to take the promotion to the next level," I said, somewhat defeated. "Looks like it's back to the drawing board for me."

With that, I said good-bye to Franny, who followed me out to prop up a new billboard next to the street in front of Mother Earth's front door. "HONK IF YOU DIG CACTI," it said, appealing to the commuting gardeners of the world. Several horns sounded in the distance as I walked back to work.

Later that evening, during the dinner shift, Lucinda called to thank me for the flowers I'd sent. "You shouldn't have, Dean. But they are beautiful. Did you get them at Mother Earth's?"

"Yep, Franny took care of me once again."

"She really knows her stuff," Lucinda said.

"She sure does," I agreed. Lucinda meant flowers, but I was referring to Franny's marketing knowledge. Her understanding of short-term marketing as it relates to long-term marketing underscored the Grill's need for planning — not the shallow level that characterized our earlier promotions, but a more in-depth

approach. I made sure to update my marketing notebook accordingly.

I was making head-way learning the funda-mentals of *Slam Dunk Marketing*, but the time had come to figure out how to put them to work effectively. For too long I'd been taking wild shots at the marketing hoop, missing more than I made. About the only thing that was going right lately was my growing relationship with Lucinda.

"Let's get together Sunday," she said just before hanging up the phone. "My place. I'll do the cooking for a change."

"I'll be there," I said. "We've got a lot to talk about."

— *"All right, agent 'Double-Oh Hamburger.' Come by my office today at 4 p.m. and we'll talk."*

## CHAPTER 6
### DEVELOPING THE GAME PLAN

Sunday couldn't have come fast enough. I had been looking forward to having a nice dinner with Lucinda. Though I'd known her for years, we'd never really gotten to know each other beyond the pleasantries exchanged whenever our paths crossed at the basketball arena. Now I was thinking there could be something more to this friendship.

I knocked on the door to her house — a brick bungalow located in the fashionable part of town. Lucinda answered wearing an apron splattered with so much red sauce that it looked like she had just painted a barn.

"Hey, there, Lucinda," I said. After handing her the bottle of Chianti I'd brought, I took notice of the stains. "Looks like we're having spaghetti."

"Lasagna," she replied.

Lucinda looked as great as always — her long dark hair pulled back in a barrette, her fresh, youthful face belying 37 years of age — but I could tell she was exasperated.

"You all right?" I asked.

"Barely," she said, straining to smile. Apparently, a few culinary misadventures had just occurred, including a cap that flew off a container of oil and vinegar as Lucinda was shaking it. I could see abstract streaks of the salad dressing painted on one of the kitchen walls, reminding me of Picasso in a strange way.

Once we sat down to eat, my dinner companion relaxed. She asked about my efforts to improve the marketing of the Red River Grill, which got me talking for the next half-hour or so. I rattled off the multitude of ideas I'd been collecting in my marketing notebook. Dozen Dozen, Name Game, the Inside-Out Approach, LSE's — Lucinda must have been puzzled at all the code words I used to record my newfound marketing knowledge. If that were the case, she didn't let on, like the good poker player she was.

"You've certainly been busy," she said. "But it sounds to me like you're in desperate need of a game plan. If you don't put one together, I'm afraid all these great ideas of yours won't get off the pages of your notebook — at least not successfully. Lack of proper planning has stung you in the past, hasn't it?"

My ego was bruised. "Hold on there, Lucinda. I've carefully planned every promotion I've tried. It just seems like the more planning I do, the more complex the event becomes, which works against its success. Sometimes I wonder if it would be better to just pull the trigger and see what happens."

"Yeah, but if you pull the trigger without aiming first, you're going to miss the target nine times out of 10," she said. "Which is pretty close to the same free-throw percentage you had in your playing days, wasn't it?"

"Very funny," I said.

There was no arguing with Lucinda. Years of sell-outs and huge revenue increases at the basketball arena illustrated her marketing success. There were often empty seats at the Red River Grill, a situation I was working harder than an organ grinder's monkey to turn around. In the restaurant business, few things are more expensive than an empty chair.

Lucinda continued with her train of thought. "There's no replacement for a well-constructed plan," she said. "The mistake a lot of people make, however, is starting from the beginning. They plan an event or promotion from A to Z, only to discover in the end that the 'Z' stands for *zero* profits because the decisions made early on didn't support a worthwhile return on investment."

"So what's the solution?" I asked. I knew all too well what 'Z' stood for.

Her answer seemed so fundamental. "The solution is to determine where you want to end up before you get going. In other words, plan your marketing in reverse," she said. "Once you have an idea, the first thing you need to do is identify your goal. What do you want to happen as a result of the promotion? Put it down on paper."

I interrupted her at that point. "OK, let me tell you what I want to happen," I said. "I've got this idea for a great promotion. You know as well as anyone there's a lot of public interest in the Wildcats right now because they're winning the big games. They even have a shot at winning the conference tournament. I'm going to take advantage of the Wildcats' winning ways and run a promotion that gets covered by the media and attracts lots of new, enthusiastic customers to the Red River Grill, many of whom will turn into regulars."

"So what's the idea?" Lucinda asked.

I couldn't wait to tell her. "Coach is bald, right?"

"Last time I checked, his head had about as much hair as a basketball," Lucinda said, unsure of where I was headed.

"What if I were to get the word out that I, owner and operator of the Red River Grill, was willing to shave my own head bald to match Coach's — on TV no less! — if the Wildcats win the conference championship?"

Lucinda was intrigued. "Go on."

"There could be special events happening at the restaurant during each one of the televised games, culminating with the head-shaving if our boys win the whole enchilada. With eight teams in the tournament, there's a possible three games the Wildcats could play on their way to the championship. I'd have something big planned each night."

"Like what?" Lucinda asked. I could tell she was not only expressing a genuine interest in the idea, but also furthering her point about the importance of preparing a marketing plan. I gave her more of the details. "I'll have drawings for prizes, special drinks, former Wildcat players hanging around signing auto-graphs, team paraphernalia hung up around the restau-rant and, the *pièce de résistance*, an authentic barber's chair set up and ready to go, if needed. I'll invite Lou from the Downtown Barbershop to do the honors."

"Sounds like a lot of hoops to jump through," Lucinda said. "What kind of R.O.I. are you looking for?"

"Hell, I don't even know how much this thing will cost yet." I was trying to be funny, but Lucinda wasn't laughing.

"Dean, I can see you're headed for disaster already," she said. "You've spent all this time dreaming up all this marketing mayhem that sounds great but may or may not be cost effective. Remember what I said earlier? You need to plan in reverse. First, project the revenue the promotion is likely to generate, then allocate a percentage of it to cover your costs — costs you've determined in advance. Don't get me wrong, Dean, I love your idea. It's the best one you've had since giving your wing-tip shoes to charity. But if you make four grand on an event that cost you five grand to pull off, you're gonna feel pretty stupid walking around town with a bald head."

I felt pretty stupid already, but I attempted to recover a pinch of pride. "Sure, sure, I'll figure it all out. I just need to decide what my return on investment should be. Any ideas?"

"Depends on your point of view," Lucinda said. "If you're after a short-term winner, it's not worth your time for anything less than a 10-dollar return on every dollar invested during the time of the promotion. If, for example, you've projected $4,000 in revenue, you'll want to spend around $400 on the event itself. On the other hand, you could get away with, say, a four-to-one return on investment if you can expect long-term benefits from the promotion — primarily repeat business from customers who took part in the event and new business created by your media exposure. It's tough to measure those things, though. You're probably better off sticking to a 10-to-one ratio on the immediate expenditures and making sure you leverage that amount for long-term benefits as well."

"For conversation's sake," I said, "let's say I know what I want to happen and I've already crunched the numbers. Then what?" I wanted to understand the whole picture.

"It's no different than what Coach does in preparing his team for an upcoming game," Lucinda said. "Every opponent is different, and Coach has to plan specific ways to counter each one's strengths and take advantage of each one's weaknesses. What may look like unstructured, run-and-gun basketball on the court is actually a well-executed game plan. You should know that better than anyone. You played for Coach for four years."

"Yeah, but the funny thing is, players usually don't take part in those planning sessions," I said. "Coach just comes to practice and says, 'Do this and do that.' Come game time, we did this and we did that. It was that simple."

Lucinda hadn't fully made her point. "Why don't you do this, Dean," she said. "Ask Coach if you can sit in on one of his game-strategy sessions. See what he does and it might give you some insight on effective planning."

My evening with Lucinda had turned into another Marketing 101 session. Before we knew it, the lasagna had gotten cold on our plates, the cheese coagulating in an unsavory manner. Our salads had become limp. The garlic bread, which Lucinda had to fetch last-minute from a nearby supermarket after burning the first loaf, had sat on the table untouched throughout our conversation.

"You know what?" she asked. "I think we should blow off this dinner and go grab some sushi instead — my treat. It's a beautiful night and we can walk to a place I know a couple of blocks away. Who knows? You might even pick up another marketing idea or two."

"Are you sure?" I asked. "You've worked so hard on everything."

"Not that hard," she said. "And, besides, one bite of that lasagna and you'd have realized what a lousy cook I am. Marketing I know. Ricotta, I don't."

"Well, then, I guess it's time for a little freshwater eel," I said. "I'm starving. Put food in front of me and it will disappear faster than fish sticks at a feline convention."

Lucinda's words of advice rang in my ears as I phoned Coach the next day to ask permission to attend a game-planning session. As a player, I'd never participated in one. Coach and his assistants did all the planning. The team would get involved later, working on the skills at practice that would put us in the best position to win. We might develop a special in-bounds play to make use of our height advantage or a special series of backdoor screens to stop less physical opponents in their tracks or special full-court presses to slow down a fast-breaking team. All devised with one desired outcome in mind — a win.

Granted, my own marketing outcomes at the Red River Grill were more complicated than a "W" in the won/loss column. But I was hopeful that Coach would give me a behind-the-scenes look at his game-preparation techniques, which he did after a little good-natured needling.

"You're not really a secret agent hired by our opponents, are you?" he asked on his end of the line.

"Well, now that you mention it, I am," I said. "But for a price I could be coaxed into becoming a double-agent and spreading disinformation that would actually benefit the Wildcats."

"All right, agent 'Double-Oh Hamburger.' Come by my office today at 4 p.m. and we'll talk."

At 4 sharp, I entered Coach's shrine. Hanging on the walls were photographs of famous celebrations after key Wildcat victories. Shelf after shelf was filled with leather basketballs autographed by past championship teams and gleaming trophies, each apparently dusted and shined on a regular basis. Coach was sitting behind an oak desk covered with player statistics, sticky notes, every business book imaginable and a team paraphernalia marketing calendar two months ahead. Coach's feet were propped up over the mess. His two assistants, stationed on either side of an old grade-school chalkboard, were busy drawing X's and O's representing what players would be coached to do in the upcoming game. The board was filled with lines, arrows, scribbles and other unintelligible marks.

I figured I was late. "You've started without me," I said. "And I'm right on time."

I shook hands with the assistants, Bo and Todd, and took a vacant chair in the corner of the office. Coach was all business. "Dean here wants to see what goes on behind closed doors," he said. "Let's get on with it. I don't want to be here all night."

What I learned that night altered my marketing mind-set. It echoed what Lucinda had said about planning in reverse. Coach, though, called it

73

"backtiming." Written on top of the chalkboard was the question: "How are we going to win this game?" Then he and his assistants worked backward from there, first identifying the position they wanted the team to be in with five minutes left in the game. They had strategies for several scenarios, built around whether they were winning or losing at the time.

Ideally, they'd like to switch to a man-to-man defense after playing zone throughout the first half and part of the second half, catching their opponent off guard. During that same period in the game, they'd change the focus of their offense, featuring the low-post players after starting off with an outside attack. They planned some surprises for early in the second half, which set up a strategy for the first half — right down to the opening tip-off. They also outlined each player's assignment and goals for performance, then established the amount of practice time it would take to prepare the team to succeed, providing sort of an R.O.I. measurement. There were even discussions about what the school band should play to pump up the team during warm-ups. Coach said he'd give the director a call and ask for a more energetic opening number.

I kept quiet during Coach's planning session until the very end. Then I asked: "Do you always work backward like that?"

"Most of the time," Coach said. "It's like what they say: 'If you don't know where you're going, how are you going to get there?'"

The point hit home with me. "You know, Coach, I think I could adopt a similar approach for marketing the Red River Grill."

"Bet you could," he said.

"Remember that new-and-improved happy hour I started a while back?" I asked.

"Sure, I remember," Coach said.

"Not a bad idea, but the problem was Kate and I planned it from front to back, just hoping the end result would be positive. Which it wasn't. Next time around I'm going to do it right."

"Glad I could help," Coach said. "I'll send you my consulting bill. You can pay it off in burgers."

"You got a deal," I said.

On the way out the door, I stopped to retrieve my marketing notebook out of my back pocket. I jotted down the abbreviation "B.T.F.P." on an empty page and wrote what it meant — "Back To Front Planning." I added several other entries, too.

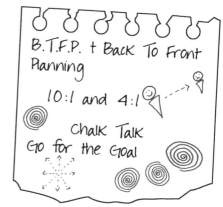

The next step would be to implement the ideas in earnest, starting with my head-shaving marketing event. First, however, I needed to consult with Kate, who was back at the Grill preparing for the dinner rush.

"Where have you been?" she asked as I walked into the restaurant. "I expected you hours ago."

"Sorry about that," I said. "I got caught up at Coach's office watching him plan for their next game."

Kate look perplexed. I had forgotten to tell her that I'd be dropping by Coach's office. Before she asked why I was there, I beat her to the punch. "I think there are a lot of parallels with what we're trying to do with our marketing efforts and what Coach and his assistants are trying to do with the Wildcat basketball team," I said. "First thing they do is ask, 'How are we going to win this game?' From there they develop a strategy in reverse, each action step supporting the outcome they want — in their case, a win."

"And in our case?" Kate asked.

"In our case, a return on investment. We need to do a better job of projecting revenue for the marketing ideas we come up with, then use that figure to determine a percentage to be used on funding the event. Lucinda, the marketing director for the Wildcats, suggests a 10-to-one return — 10 bucks for every one invested during the time of the promotion. Too often we swallow the up-front costs with little or no idea if we'll turn a profit. Optimism is no substitute for intelligent planning."

"So what do we do about it?" Kate asked.

"For starters, reverse the way we've done things in the past, starting with the idea I was telling you about the other day."

"The one where you shave your head to look like Coach's?"

"That's the one," I said.

Kate and I set a date to lay the foundation for the promotion, following the backtiming guidelines I'd picked up over the last couple of days. There was a lot to do, but I felt more confident than ever before. Having realized that improper planning can ruin a great marketing idea, I was beginning to get a hold of that elusive greased pig known as "results."

For all I knew, each of my previous marketing ideas had been fantastically conceived — just poorly executed. I wasn't as dumb as I thought I was. In the excitement of the moment, however, I forgot to knock on wood.

— *"Well, they were really on a roll in the first half," he said. "But in this game anything can happen in the second half. It's not over till it's over."*

## CHAPTER 7
### EXECUTING THE GAME PLAN

About a month before the start of the conference basketball tournament — scheduled to take place in town at Wildcat Arena — I began working with Kate to plan the Red River Grill's best promotion ever. There were many details to consider, based not only on what I had learned recently about backtiming and return on investment, but also on the other slam-dunk principles I'd picked up and recorded in my marketing notebook. Kate and I were determined to implement as many of the ideas as possible.

It was April 1 — April Fool's Day — but the irony would go unnoticed as Kate and I got down to business. Our planning session resembled the one Coach and his assistants had orchestrated in front of me, but instead of a chalkboard, Kate and I used a flip chart and multi-colored markers.

Our first order of business was to identify the main goals for the promotion, then work backward from there. The temptation at this point was to attempt too much, reaching for the stars and complicating what was reasonably achievable. To our credit, we eventually settled on two manageable objectives:

First, generate enough customer traffic to produce a 10-to-one return on investment.

Second, but no less important, get those customers to come back for a return visit.

Using a blue marker, Kate wrote our primary and secondary objectives atop the first page of the flip chart. Then, referring to the entries in my marketing notebook, we selected the ones that would help get us to where we wanted to go, listing them in no particular order. Through brainstorming, these ideas evolved into the following strategies:

*The big event.* The promotion itself revolved around my vow to shave my head if the Wildcats should win the eight-team, three-day conference tournament at the end of the month. The shaving would take place one hour after the end of the championship game, giving those who were in attendance enough time to get to the restaurant for the festivities and allowing TV crews the opportunity to set up a live link for the 10 p.m. news. As long as the Wildcats stayed alive in the tournament, they'd tip off at 7:05 p.m. each night. There was the possibility, of course, that the team could lose its first game, putting an end to the promotion after only one round. It was a risk we were willing to take because the Wildcats, the top seed and keepers of the home-court advantage, appeared to be a lock to win their first two match-ups and reach the champion-ship. So we planned on three consecutive nights for the promotion — Thursday, Friday and Saturday — know-ing we'd pull the plug if the Wildcats happened to lose early. We'd place an old-time barber's chair near the Grill's big-screen TV, to remind guests of what's to come if the team wins it all. Each night during the game, we'd run a happy hour of sorts, offering large beers for the price of a small, available only when the Wildcats are winning. We'd also encourage guests to fill out raffle tickets, including their name, address and phone number, for drawings to take place after each slam dunk by the home team. Most of the prizes would be food-and-beverage offers geared to generate repeat business at a future date. The grand prize, awarded only if the Wildcats won the championship, would be a catered party at the Red River Grill, including a keg of craft-beer and enough grub to feed 40 people. During halftimes of the games, I'd personally interview former Wildcat players at a table set up with microphones and positioned in the corner of the restaurant adjacent to the TV and barber's chair. We'd make the barber's chair available for photo opportunities, with or without me in the picture.

*External marketing.* To get the word out, we'd send out a press release describing the event in a way that piqued the interest of editors and producers at the local media outlets, including TV-news stations and every daily and weekly newspaper in the area. We'd also design a flyer around a photograph of me sitting in the barber's chair with an uneasy look on my face. The headline, in big, bold letters, would read: "WHY IS THIS GUY WORRIED?" The copy would go on to

explain how I, owner and operator of the Red River
Grill, had vowed to shave my head to match Coach's
shiny dome if the Wildcats take the championship
trophy. Why such a drastic measure? Because, long
ago, Coach had made a similar promise to shave his
head if the team *I* was playing on at the time won the
championship, which it did. After the buzz cut, however, Coach's hair never grew back. The gesture to
shave my own head was my way of showing gratitude
for Coach's sacrifice. In addition to explaining the
reason behind the promotion, the flyer would invite
ticketless customers to the Grill each night to watch
the tournament unfold on big-screen TV and enjoy
food-and-beverage specials, prize giveaways, and
conversation with former Wildcat players who'd be
joining in the fun. We'd hang the flyer around the
restaurant and train servers to call guests' attention to
it. Since Lou, owner of the Downtown Barbershop,
had already agreed to supply the old barber's chair for
the promotion and do the honors of shaving my head if
necessary, we'd mention his business in the marketing
copy and ask him to hang a flyer in his shop. We'd also
worked a deal with a nearby sporting goods store to
provide 30 basketballs per night — each signed by the
team and available to drawing winners for only $20.
The money collected would go toward the purchase of
new uniforms for the pep band.

*Internal marketing.* I had learned from Coach at the
health club that what you do *externally* to attract customers isn't as important as what you do *internally* to
get them to come back. Kate and I, while discussing
ways to generate repeat business, coined the phrase
"Make Me Feel Important," which we considered to be

the secret to treating guests and encouraging their return visits. To make our guests feel important, we'd put to use the point-and-shoot camera I'd recently purchased, taking pictures of people having a good time at the event, then framing the best ones and pinning them up on our new Wall of Fame. People would come back to see themselves spotlighted at the Red River Grill — their home away from home. And they'd bring along their friends. We'd even send copies of the photos to V.I.P.'s to remind them of the great time they had. It would also be important to prepare our staff to exceed the expectations raised in our marketing materials. At daily pre-shift meetings, we'd review details of the promotion, testing employees on their knowledge of the prizes to be given away and the food-and-beverage specials we'd be running, and using a new manager's guide we'd purchased to role play ways to maximize the service and sales potential at each customer contact point. Last but not least, we'd seek employees' commitment to the promotion's success.

*Personal marketing.* Face to face, eye to eye — this is the avenue we'd take to turn newcomers to the restaurant into regulars. Just like Lou in his barbershop, we'd make every attempt to learn and use guests' names. Credit cards would be a likely source for the information, but we'd also train staff members to introduce themselves to guests, then say: "And you are...?" They could either memorize the names or write them on the notepad inside their Server Caddies, which were provided to us by a major beer company. There'd also be an emphasis placed on performing LSE's — Little Something Extras that let guests know you're taking care of them. We'd hang up their coats, pull out their chairs, anticipate their every need.

*One-Two Marketing.* As Lucinda taught me in the sky box at Wildcat Arena, no promotion is an end in itself. In other words, it's not enough to attract customers. You have to sell them something while they're there — and do it in a way that enhances their experience. For the purposes of the head-shaving promotion, we'd aggressively pursue appetizer sales, add-on sales with entrees, and upgrades for beer, wine and cocktail orders. Once again, this would require staff training. All of sudden, a month didn't seem like a whole lot of time, but it's all we had. We would purchase and implement a turn-key video-training program called "CheckBusters: The Art of Smart Selling," which would show our staff how to improve service, build check averages and take home more tips through suggestive selling.

*Short- and long-term marketing.* During my visit with Franny at Mother Earth Flowers, she underscored the importance of creating short-term marketing opportunities that, one by one, add up to long-term success. To that end, Kate and I decided to employ a bounceback approach during the event in an attempt to increase traffic during traditionally slow days at the restaurant. Among the prizes given away would be offers for a free dessert and some for a free appetizer with the purchase of an entree, redeemable Monday through Thursday. We'd also create an atmosphere — by adding team paraphernalia to the decor and offering 99-cent margaritas to guests who show ticket stubs —

that positions the Red River Grill as *the place* to watch Wildcat games and celebrate their victories.

*Guest feedback.* Kate and I would also take the opportunity to solicit feedback as we worked the dining room during the promotion. "How are we doing?" would be the thrust of our information-gathering. We'd maintain a visible presence in the dining room, getting to know guests, introducing ourselves, handing out business cards. "If there's anything we can ever do for you," we'd say, "just let us know." Who knows what might come from this friendly gesture? We'd also gather as many business cards as possible from customers, then incorporate the information into our database.

Once Kate and I fleshed out our strategies, it was clear we had a lot of work to do. We wondered if we could do it all under budget, given our objective to achieve a 10-to-one return on investment. To find out, we projected sales for the three days of the promotion. If the media covered it like we thought they would, coupled with the Wildcat mania that had a grip on the town, we figured we could count on an additional 150 customers per night, half of whom would probably order dinner and a drink or two. The other half would probably be content drinking several beers, cocktails or specialty drinks, and perhaps sampling an appetizer. Either way, we'd be looking at a per-person check average in the $12 range, a number we'd have to call on our servers and bartenders to solidify at the point of purchase.

If we indeed managed to attract 150 customers above the normal crowd each night and maintained a $12 check average, we'd bring in an extra $1,800 a night, which indicated that our marketing budget should be $180 a night — or $540 for the whole event. That didn't sound like much. But, item by item, we calculated the potential costs of the promotion as best we could, to see if we were biting off more than we could chew.

> *The barber's chair:* Lou let us borrow it for free, but we would have to have it delivered and then returned for a cost of $45 each way. TOTAL: **$90**

> *Microphone and speaker rental:* $25 per day. TOTAL: **$75**

> Raffle tickets: $9.95 per roll. Probably need two rolls. TOTAL: **$19.90**

> *Prizes to be awarded after each slam dunk:* $4.25 each, including costs for a coupon-like card and food cost on a free dessert or appetizer with purchase of an entree. Probably hand out five per night. TOTAL: **$63.75.**

> *Grand prize:* One keg of beer plus enough food for 40 people. Our cost: $4 a head. TOTAL: **$160**

> *99-cent margarita special:* For guests who have ticket stubs. Limit one per guest and good only the night of the game shown on the ticket. Cost: $35 to produce table tents describing the offer. TOTAL: **$35**

*Development and distribution of press releases:* An estimated $90 in labor cost and $10 in postage costs. TOTAL: **$100**

*Development of flyer:* $100 to have photograph taken, $25 in printing costs. TOTAL: **$125**

*Point-and-shoot camera:* $129, but its cost could be amortized over future promotions involving the Wall of Fame. TOTAL: **$129**

*Film:* $45. Developing: $50. TOTAL: **$95**

*Training:* $149 for the video CheckBusters: The Art of Smart Selling; $30 for a manager's guide to conducting role-play exercises; and $130 in labor costs for one hour for staff to complete the training session. TOTAL: **$309**

*Comps for former Wildcat players:* We'd invite a different person each night to be interviewed at half time and comment on the game. In exchange, we'd buy their drinks and dinner. Estimated cost: $20 per night. TOTAL: **$60** (We hoped they'd each bring at least three paying friends, so this cost might actually pay for itself.)

*Team paraphernalia:* To add to the decor. TOTAL: **$25**

Kate and I didn't factor in the labor cost of our planning and executing the promotion, and we knew that we had likely missed some hidden costs as well. Yet, our first calculation of the total cost surprised us. The initial figure was $1,286.65 — well above the $540

mark that would all but guarantee us a 10-to-one
return on investment.

We had no choice but to back off on the promotion,
cutting corners wherever possible. First to go was the
team paraphernalia expense ($25), followed by the
delivery charge for the barber's chair ($90) and the
photography expense ($100). I'd pick up the chair
myself, borrowing a truck from my next-door neighbor,
and I recalled that one of my employees was studying
photography in school and could shoot the picture at
no cost as a class project. We also decided not to factor
in the camera purchase ($129) or the film and develop-
ing expense ($95), because we'd use the camera for
years to come and the Wall of Fame photos would pay
for themselves as guests returned to see the display.

Even with those cuts, however, we still needed to
pare down the total by another $307.65, which just
happened to be in the ballpark of the training expense
($309). Instead of purchasing the materials and spend-
ing the hour with our employees to complete the
training, we'd develop our own suggestive-selling tips
and practice them, time permitting, in the daily pre-
shift meetings we already had scheduled to review
details of the upcoming promotion.

Bingo! Kate and I had identified the essentials of
the promotion along with the marketing strategies —
internal and external — that would make it a success.
We'd determined a budget that would ensure a minimum 10-to-one return on investment. Now all we
needed to do was backtime each step of the execution
process starting with tip-off of the championship game

— 7:05 p.m. on Saturday, April 29 — then working in reverse, day by day, to plot every step needed to pull off the event.

We tried to keep it as simple as possible. For each day, we detailed only the task, the person responsible for completing the task and the time by which the task should be completed. April 27 and 26, the day of and the day before the start of the promotion, looked like this:

**April 27:**

*Sid* and *John* to set up interviewing table, making sure microphones and speakers work. Also need to position the barber's chair to the right of the TV and in front of the internal Red River Grill sign. That way all photos will have the sign in the background. (10 a.m.)

*Jessie* to set up fishbowl in front of hostess stand, placing the rules card and a roll of raffle tickets nearby (10 a.m.)

**April 26:**

*Kate* to double check delivery of extra food and beverage ordered to accommodate 150-person increase in traffic. (Before noon.)

*Dean* to follow up with first former Wildcat player scheduled to be interviewed, making sure he's going to be there on time tomorrow. Need to call each player two days before the morning of their appearance. (10 a.m.)

These were just two days. Kate and I established mini-action plans for *each* day from April 2 through the end of the tournament on April 29 — an arduous but rewarding job that forced us to think through each detail of what needed to be done. Later, when we looked at the multitude of tasks all at once, the work ahead seemed overwhelming. We found it comforting to narrow our focus to one day at a time, confident our step-by-step planning would keep us on track.

To keep a record of our process — one Kate and I could refer to in the future — I kept a history of the daily tasks in my marketing notebook. I also made some backtiming notes, drawing on the insights Coach and his assistants had given me at the chalk talk.

As expected, the Wildcats went into the tournament as the top seed. As expected, the media responded enthusiastically to our press releases, broadcasting and publishing story after story about the event. I was interviewed at least a dozen times, and business at the restaurant picked up by almost 20 percent a week before the promotion even began. I couldn't help but think this could be the *Slam Dunk Marketing* promotion we'd been striving for.

The night of the Wildcats' first tournament game, at 7:05 p.m. sharp, the basketball went up on the big-screen TV and a packed house at the Red River Grill cheered on the home team in unison. It was busier than Kate or I had imagined it would be. Guests filled every table and stood three-deep at the bar. Our servers appeared to be a bit frazzled and the cooks were running behind, but the dollar signs in my eyes prevented me from seeing any problems.

The Wildcats led every second of the first half, meaning we had to honor the large-beer special without a break. There had also been an inordinate amount of slam dunks — at least 10 — and we were depleting the promotional items faster than expected. No matter, the place was hoppin'.

With the Wildcats winning the game by 15 points, I sat down at the interviewing table to chat with our first halftime guest, Russell Jones, who 10 years ago had started at center on one of Coach's many championship teams.

"So, Russell," I began. "How are the Wildcats looking."

"Well, they were really on a roll in the first half," he said. "But in this game anything can happen in the second half. It's not over till it's over."

Little did I know that Russell could have been talking about the potential success of our promotion.

*— I'd soon find out that bald can be beautiful —
as well as a lot of other things.*

## CHAPTER 8
### FINISHING WHAT YOU STARTED

In the second half of the opening game, the Wild-cats squandered their 15-point lead, but held on to win by four. The crowd glued to the big-screen TV at the Red River Grill roared with enthusiasm as time ran out and the buzzer sounded. At that point, about half of the guests, especially the ones standing around the bar, finished their drinks and headed out the door. The rest remained at their tables, which from my vantage seemed more bare than they should be.

After all, Kate and I had spent considerable time before the promotion training the staff to suggestively sell appetizers and upgrade liquor orders to make up for the profit margins we'd narrowed on the food and beverage specials available during the game. But there was only minimal evidence of consumed Shrimp Baskets, Quesadillas, Cheese Sticks and the like, which was worrisome because the raucous group of guests had warded off diners not interested in the basketball game, and the fans we did have at the tables were nursing

93

drinks but not ordering anything to go with them — at least not as much as I had wanted.

What's more, I had specifically asked our servers and bartenders to invite guests back for each night the Wildcats remained alive in the conference tournament. I didn't hear a single invitation. Apparently the staff had forgotten my instructions in the hustle and bustle of delivering food and drinks, reconciling tabs and staying out of the weeds. Figuring most guests knew enough about the promotion to come back the next night anyway, I put off reminding the staff to offer those invitations and, ultimately, didn't do it.

Guests filled out a lot of raffle tickets for the prize drawings held after each slam dunk. Only one problem: Many weren't completed in full, which would thwart efforts to input the information into our database. I realized too late what should have been done in the first place — servers needed to make sure each guest's raffle ticket was complete before throwing it into the fish-bowl. But I had overlooked that part of executing the game plan. I'd be sure to follow up with the staff before the second night of the promotion.

There was some good news. A producer for one of the local news stations called to schedule an interview with me on Friday afternoon. The story would be part of a pre-game package aired that night, giving me an opportunity to generate some traffic for the restaurant and remind the viewing public of my vow to go bald if the Wildcats should win it all. The publicity would also set the table for live coverage of the head-shaving event, broadcast by not only this particular station, but also the others in town.

My upcoming 15 minutes of fame led me to shuffle my priorities. Instead of following up right away with my staff to encourage appetizer sales, liquor upgrades and properly filled-out raffle tickets, I spent the bulk of Friday preparing for the TV interview. I changed my clothes half a dozen times and parted my hair on the left, then on the right, then back on the left. I polished the barber's chair, which is where I'd be sitting during the interview. I rehearsed with Kate the traffic-building language I would ingeniously weave into my on-air responses. Then I anxiously waited alone for the reporter to arrive.

While waiting, I flipped through my marketing notebook and saw the entries "One-Two Traffic" and "Power of Personal, Personal, Personal!" In a burst of inspiration, I called six of the eight local radio stations, inviting them to cover the head-shaving event.

By that time, the TV reporter had arrived, along with a cameraman who was all business. He positioned me in the barber's chair, adjusting its height and the angle he'd be shooting it from, then turned on a hot, white light affixed to the top of the camera. Looking into the lens, I imagined a million people hanging on every word I'd say, which caused me to perspire all the more. The reporter instructed me to look straight at her during the interview and try not to be nervous. Was it obvious?

Then she said, with the videotape rolling: "We're here with Dean 'Baggy Sox' McBride, former Wildcats basketball player and now owner of the Red River Grill, where Saturday night he's promised to shave his head if the Wildcats win the championship. Dean, why lose your locks?"

This reporter knew her stuff. I had no idea how she found out my playing-days nickname — one I hated, by the way — but I managed to answer the question with only minor hems and haws. "For one thing, it's out of respect and admiration all of us at the Red River Grill have for the great job Coach has done this year with such a young team," I said, nodding to the camera. "But also because — most fans don't know this — Coach used to have more hair than John Travolta in *Saturday Night Fever*. That is until he made a similar vow to shave his head if the team I was playing on at the time won the championship, which we did. That was 1973. Only problem was, Coach's hair never grew back. He's been bald as a hard-boiled egg ever since. Now it's pay-back time, and I'm happy to do it if the Wildcats can do it."

The reporter asked several other questions, but my first response was the only one that was used in the story. Good thing I emphasized the restaurant's name on camera. We watched the interview on our big-screen TV, much to the delight of the guests who had arrived early to get a table and watch the pre-game show. It dawned on me, however, that it was no longer possible to meet with my front-of-the-house employees and shore up their service and sales techniques, which were missing in action the night before. Somehow I hoped that everything would just take care of itself.

It didn't. Word of mouth generated from the first-night guests combined with the TV coverage sent droves into the Red River Grill to watch the second-round game. It was all the servers and bartenders could do to keep up with the drink orders, and they were falling behind at that. Some guests had frustrated looks burned onto their faces, others were braving the four-deep backup at the bar, waving bills at the bartenders and shouting out orders the staff couldn't hear. So much for the well-intentioned plan to bowl guests over with the quality of our service. Instead of "little something extra," LSE stood for "little service expected" on this busy Saturday night. Coach had once told me: "Good marketing can kill a marginal business." He was right.

I was beginning to think that I just couldn't win, which wasn't the case for the Wildcats who were on their way to a blowout victory. Once again, the number of slam dunks reached double-digits, further depleting our drawing giveaways. Fortunately, most of the prizes were bounceback offers, inviting guests to enjoy a free dessert or appetizer with the purchase of an entree the next time they came in. Still, we'd given away far more than planned. Our 10-to-one return on investment was in jeopardy.

Kate and I, rushing around the dining room like horseflies on a road apple, exchanged glances midway through the second half of the game. Our expressions revealed a mix of mutual panic and fatigue, but there was little we could do at the moment — except keep the guests' beer glasses full and our heads above water. We had made promising strides in our marketing efforts, reaching the point where our sound ideas had been carefully planned and executed up until the moment of truth. But I didn't have to talk with Coach, Lou, Franny or Lucinda to understand there was a missing element in our game plan: We hadn't finished what we started.

Sure, Kate and I had asked employees to upsell food and beverage orders and even given them some tips to succeed. But, push come to shove, they had scant motivation to follow through on the dining-room floor, especially under pressure. I recalled that when I was employed in corporate America, many years ago, our company's salespeople normally worked for commission on product they sold, and often received motivation in the form of sales contests. It was the logical approach.

As the Wildcats wrapped up their second win in a row, I was determined, if possible, to draw on my own experiences to salvage the profitability of this promotion. I'd start by running a Saturday night sales contest for my own salespeople — particularly the Grill's servers and bartenders. It also occurred to me that they're on commission, too, earning 10 to 15 percent in tips on each guest check. If they'd commit themselves to providing customer-pleasing LSE's and building per-person check averages, their tips would dramatically increase. Front-of-the-house employees who under-stand what's in it for them to excel at sales and service are bound to do a better job.

Saturday morning Kate and I prepared a last-minute call to arms, which we'd deliver to the staff in a pre-shift meeting at 4:30 p.m. On a flip chart, we outlined the rules for a sales contest entitled "Tic Tac Toe," which we pulled out of the book "Playing Games at Work: 52 Incentives, Contests and Rewards." In each square of a standard Tic Tac Toe grid, we listed the number of a specific appetizer, add-on or beverage that must be sold in order for servers to mark it out. In the upper left-hand square, for example, it said: "5 Shrimp Baskets." In the middle square, it said: "10 Margaritas." Each square contained a sales requirement, some tougher to achieve than others, but all designed to promote high-profit menu items.

The first server to get a Tic Tac Toe — three squares marked out in a straight or diagonal line — would not have to do his or her sidework for a month. Kate and I would assume the responsibility during that time. The second-prize winner would receive his or her choice of shifts for two weeks. Third prize would be choice of shifts for one week. Following the book's suggestion to make everyone a winner, we'd also liberally hand out lottery tickets for each employee's million-dollar effort.

In addition to the sales contest, we'd run an incentive to encourage all front-of-the-house employees to perform those little something extras that wow guests and generate repeat business. Any time Kate or I spotted someone going the extra mile to pamper guests, we'd write that person's name on a piece of paper and enter it into a drawing to take place after the Saturday night shift. Grand prize would be $50 — a generous amount we hoped would demonstrate the importance we placed on providing uncommon service.

Another shortcoming in the first two nights of the promotion was our staff's forgetfulness in inviting guests back for a return visit. Kate came up with an idea to rectify the situation. Instead of trying to be unobtrusive with the point-and-shoot camera, she'd get in the middle of the action, shooting photograph after photograph of the cheering Wildcat fans. Afterward, servers, bartenders and greeters could inform guests that many of the pictures would go up on a special Wall of Fame featuring Wildcat fans. The return-visit dialogue might go something like: "You'll have to come back and see yourself in the spotlight." To make sure the message gets delivered consistently, Kate and I would simply demand that every table and the front row of the bar hear it. Period. We'd tell the staff: "It's your job to get it done." To get the anchor photos needed to create extra customer excitement about being on the Wall of Fame, I'd invite the players and Coach in for a free victory meal at a later date. We'd take pictures of the team posing with customers — the fans.

Finally, I would show everyone some raffle tickets from the previous two nights, ones lacking enough information — an address here, a last name there — to be useful additions to our database. The short-term marketing opportunity was to encourage guests to redeem their free dessert or appetizer offer on a future visit. But equally, if not more important, was the long-term angle to send personal, targeted mailings to recipients already familiar with the Red River Grill.

As one last incentive, I'd ask servers to put their name in the lower right-hand corner of each raffle ticket they collected and deposited in the fishbowl. For each winner pulled out in the drawings, I'd also award

$2 to the server whose name appeared in the corner — but only if the ticket were completed correctly.

I recorded the follow-up steps Kate and I had devised in my marketing notebook.

Employees entered Saturday's pre-shift meeting dragging their heels, still trying to recover from the break-neck pace of the promotion's first two nights. Mention of the sales contest and the LSE and raffle-ticket incentives, however, raised their spirits tremendously. There was also a moment of enlightenment when I used examples in a book called "Service That Sells!" to illustrate how their tips represent a 10 to 15 percent commission that grows in step with increasing guest-check averages. I knew in an instant that the opportunity for staff members to take home prizes and pocket more tips was just the ticket to finish what we had started on a positive note. After I promised to include photos of employees, they agreed to zealously plug the Wall of Fame, promoting repeat visits come hell or high water.

We didn't dare ask for any more extra output at this, the 11th hour. It was championship game night. Our offensive attack had been drawn up. A lot was riding on our ability — borrowing some of Coach's chalk-talk lingo — to set the right screens, make all the right passes and go in for a slam dunk, whether the Wildcats win the whole enchilada or not.

With tip-off only minutes away, the pieces magically fell into place. I witnessed a server handing a raffle ticket back to a guest. "We need to get your phone number, too," she said, pointing to the empty line.

I overheard one of our bartenders suggesting and successfully selling an appetizer. "It's more fun to eat at the bar than drink at a table," he was saying. "Our Shrimp Baskets are really popular, but my favorite is the Quesadilla with smoked chicken added to it."

Another server was realizing how easy it is to upgrade a cocktail order and upgrade her tips in the process. "Would you like to try Cuervo Gold in your margarita?" she asked. The guests at the table enthusiastically went along with the recommendation.

I even got into the action. "What's with the camera?" a guest inquired when Kate took a picture of him whooping it up with his friends. "It's for a special Wall of Fame where we're going to honor friends of the Wildcats and the Red River Grill," I said. "You'll have to come back and see yourself in the spotlight. It should be up in about a week."

The fact that I was willing to practice what I had preached inspired the rest of the staff to follow suit. As the night progressed, guests throughout the restaurant were jockeying for position in front of Kate's camera, hoping to earn recognition on the Wall of Fame. It was amazing how a little follow-up with employees and the power of our own personal marketing efforts created such big results.

The Wildcats, meanwhile, were leading their opponent, the loathed Mustangs, by several baskets with five minutes left in the title game. As always, Coach was pacing the sideline, demanding an all-out effort on defense and spreading out the offense to eat up time on the clock and set up a backdoor lane to the hoop. At this juncture in the game, he was looking to his players for a high-percentage slam dunk. So was I at the Red River Grill.

Crews from the local TV stations had arrived by 9:30 p.m., anticipating a Wildcat victory and a soon-to-be-bald restaurant owner. Grinning from ear to ear, I took a seat in the barber's chair located strategically in front of the internal Red River Grill sign and shook hands with Lou who, standing behind me, was ready to go, a comb in one hand and the electric razor in the other.

Excitement in the restaurant reached roof-trembling levels as the final seconds ticked off in the game and the winning Wildcats rushed onto the basketball court, greeted by delirious fans cascading down from the stands. You couldn't hear a thing on the big-screen TV — not over the rowdy fans screaming and high-fiving from the bar to the dining room. The TV camera operators flipped on their bright lights and began recording the pandemonium.

It's at this point that Coach, back at the arena, did me the biggest favor in the world — a secret plot he and I had arranged earlier in the week to help the Red River Grill deliver a one-two marketing knockout punch. When reporters approached him after the victory, he initially ducked questions about the game and instead plugged the head-shaving event.

"I'll answer all your questions in a second," he told reporters. "But first I want to see my good friend Dean, the owner of the Red River Grill, make good on his promise to shave his head if we won the championship. And, boy, did we win."

The TV stations had no choice but to patch into the festivities in progress at the Grill. Drawing on the wisdom contained in my marketing notebook, I successfully delayed the head-shaving until Coach appeared on a live feed, which several of the stations put into a split screen — Coach on one side, me on the other — which our own guests could watch on the big-screen TV. It was Coach, in fact, who gave Lou the barber the official go-ahead to rev up the clippers.

This one-two punch netted the restaurant almost seven minutes of prime-time coverage and allowed our servers to refill drinks and put in extra orders for appetizers. Entertained and well-fed, guests would end up sticking around for at least an hour after the game was over. I also stalled the proceedings long enough to serve some complimentary shrimp and specialty frozen drinks to the reporters who, in between bites on air, would provide an unspoken endorsement of our food and beverage. Kate was busy photographing the TV and radio crews enjoying themselves for our Wall of Fame.

Eventually, all attention turned to me. Reporters on the scene were saying: "We're live. We're live." And they began filing reports to viewers watching at home. I couldn't resist playing to the crowd. "How 'bout those Wildcats!" I tried to shout above the noise, but it was no use. An eerie chant, starting low then building toward a deafening volume, had swallowed all other sounds in the restaurant.

"Cut it off! Cut it off! Cut it off!" The words even silenced the reporters. It seemed everyone wanted blood — or at least hair!

Lou, his own adrenaline pumping, fired up the electric razor. The place went wild, and I wondered if I'd live to tell the tale. The first pass of the razor took off a big chunk of hair, which floated peacefully to the ground where it was stomped into oblivion by rowdies bullying their way up front for a closer look.

As the razor's second pass created a wind tunnel through my scalp, I mused to myself: "Oh, the things I've done to achieve *Slam Dunk Marketing* success." I also began to wonder if my hair would ever grow back. I'd soon find out that bald can be beautiful — as well as a lot of other things.

— *"What do you mean —*
*walking, talking billboards?"*

## CHAPTER 9
### WALKING, TALKING BILLBOARDS

Some men look good with a bald head. Coach, Kareem Abdul-Jabbar and Mahatma Gandhi all spring to mind. My own absence of hair, however, made me look like an escapee from an insane asylum. Small children on bicycles veered away from me. Dogs growled. Even in my own neighborhood, the insecure dead-bolted their front doors whenever I approached.

I didn't care. The last night of the conference-tournament promotion was a resounding success — not enough of one to earn a 10-to-one return on investment, but more than enough to make up for the execution shortcomings we'd experienced the first two nights. When it was all said and done, Kate and I figured we'd cleared nearly eight bucks for every one spent.

And who knows? We could still reach 10-to-one down the road if guests redeemed the many bounceback offers we handed out and were receptive, upon their return visit, to our servers' suggestive-selling techniques. Kate and I, now committed to providing regular staff training, had scheduled several hour-long sessions, in addition to daily pre-shift team meetings, to emphasize the importance of selling extras and add-ons to guests who come in to redeem special offers — and getting the job done in a way that exceeds expectations and enhances perceived quality of service.

The weeks following the Wildcats' championship victory, hoop hysteria was in evidence from one end of town to the other. You couldn't walk down any street without seeing fans wearing team T-shirts, sweatshirts and ballcaps. Anywhere the public gathered — from the coffee shops to the grocery stores — the conversations taking place almost always had something to do with the winning Wildcats. The TV stations were running story after story about the title victory. Coach was given the key to the city.

Now that's *Slam Dunk Marketing* success! And the person responsible for it — outside of Coach and his basketball players, of course — was the Wildcats' marketing director and my hope-to-be girlfriend, Lucinda. We met over dinner one night to congratulate each other on our mutual successes. It was at a Chinese restaurant called the Blue Dragon.

"Well, you're finally going to get some time off," I said after Lucinda and I had taken our seats. "And deservedly so."

"I can't wait," Lucinda said. "I don't know for sure if I was busier before or after the championship. It's really been a whirlwind, with all the press coverage and public attention. Part of me is glad the hype is starting to quiet down."

"I don't know about that," I said. "The Wildcats are still the talk of the town, and it seems like wherever I look these days I see team clothing proudly worn by fans, young and old."

"Yeah, they're our walking, talking billboards. And they don't charge us a cent for all the exposure."

"What do you mean — walking, talking billboards?" I asked. Sensing the arrival of another important lesson, I took out the marketing notebook from my back pocket.

"They're just that," Lucinda explained. "They're customers who, free of charge, advertise your business just because they're thrilled with its products or they think it's cool to let others know they're your fans. The billboard can be figurative, as in the case of customers talking about and therefore spreading positive word of mouth about your company. Or it can be literal, as in the case of customers wearing T-shirts, sweatshirts and ballcaps bearing your company's logo. If you can create both forms of billboards, you may never need to purchase any awareness-building ads again. Everybody will know who you are. You got a great start with all the free publicity you received during the head-shaving event."

"I'm a little confused," I said. "Wasn't it you who tried to talk me out of producing Red River Grill T-shirts during my fruitless happy-hour promotion?"

"The difference is, you were giving them away back then — every one of them. It's funny. People generally place more value in something they have to pay for or would have had to pay for if they hadn't received it as a prize. During your happy-hour promotion, if you had T-shirts already for sale, say $15 each, then awarded a few of them as giveaways, recipients would have said: 'Wow, I won a $15 T-shirt, and it's really cool.' Establishing the price point enhances customers' perceived value, and it provides you with another profit-center opportunity in your restaurant."

I stopped her right there. "Yeah, but selling T-shirts isn't as easy as it sounds. I speak from experience."

As always, Lucinda was one step ahead of me. "I agree," she said. "That's why you have to create an environment in which the T-shirts sell themselves. Do you think anybody would be wearing Wildcat stuff if the team was a snore to watch or lost most of its games? Not a chance. Same goes for the Red River Grill. If it's just another restaurant and loses more often than not in the customer-service game, nobody's going to give a hoot about your lousy T-shirts, let alone spread positive word of mouth about your operation."

"Point taken," I said. "So what do I have to do to create that environment?"

"You're well on your way," Lucinda said. "You're taking steps to upgrade your service delivery, which in itself will help separate the Grill from the rest of the pack. Plus, your cameo on every 10 o'clock news program identified the Grill as an 'in' place to be. Now you just need to reinforce those images with the repeat customers you've been generating."

The obvious question at this juncture in our conversation was: "How?"

"Staying busy is a good place to start," Lucinda said. "Nobody wants to eat in an empty restaurant. It's disconcerting, to say the least. You wonder: 'Is it the food?' And if there are only a few tables filled, it sends the message to incoming guests that this isn't a popular place to eat. So what I'm saying is, you're doing the right thing to build traffic and generate repeat business, because they'll keep the place active."

Even in the best of times, however, restaurants have slow shifts — a fact that I was quick to point out to Lucinda. She understood, relating how even the popular Wildcats had a few poorly attended games, particularly in the preseason against weaker, lower-division teams.

"You'll notice," she said, "that most of the cameras covering those games are facing the stands where the majority of our fans sit. It creates the illusion the stadium is packed, even if there are lots of empty seats out of the camera's view. You can do the same thing in your restaurant. When it's slow, have your greeters seat tables in bunches, especially near windows. It'll create a better first impression for arriving guests."

"Great idea!" I said. "I'll try it tomorrow. But let's get back to creating walking, talking billboards. Is that all there is to it — keeping the seats filled and selling T-shirts?"

"It's a little more complicated than that," Lucinda said. "Don't forget all those notes you've got written down in that marketing notebook of yours. They won't do you any good unless you use them!"

By this time, our entrees had arrived. I ordered the Sesame Chicken. Lucinda was trying the Spicy Beef. Her first bite, hot as a mouthful of coals, kept her from speaking until she could extinguish the fire with the house special Green Tea.

"Hot?" I asked.

"You could say that," she said with a cough, tears welling up in her eyes.

Once Lucinda gathered her composure, she tried a little experiment. "What's the best movie theater in town?" she asked out of the blue.

"Oh, I don't know," I said, not catching on immediately. "I guess it would be the Egyptian Theater?"

"Why the Egyptian?" Lucinda probed.

I thought about the question for a while, then said: "Well, they've preserved a sense of history there. The theater has charm — unlike the multitude of cineplexes that have sprouted up like weeds everywhere."

"OK," Lucinda said, "what's the best coffee shop in town?"

"What are you getting at?"

"Just answer the question!" Lucinda insisted.

"The best coffee shop... that would have to be Uncommon Grounds, over in Asbury Park."

"Why Uncommon Grounds?" Lucinda asked, holding to the pattern.

"I like the fact that they have a lot of old library books lying around for customers to read, and their fresh-fruit desserts are outrageous."

"All right, my third and last question is, 'What's the best restaurant in town?'"

"The Red River Grill, of course," I said without hesitating.

"Why the Red River Grill?"

Strangely enough, it was a question I wasn't fully prepared to answer. I could have mentioned our food, but a lot of restaurants in town offer good food, especially in the brew-and-burger niche. Atmosphere? The riverfront decor did produce its share of favorable comments, but, shoot, even the greasy fish-and-chips joint down the street had old boat oars and funky aquatic taxidermy on the wall. Lucinda could see that I was stuck.

"I think we've learned a couple things from this exercise," she said. "One, whether you know it or not, you're a walking, talking billboard for the Egyptian Theater and the Uncommon Grounds coffee shop. If any of your guests ask for recommendations on where to see a movie or grab an early morning cappuccino, you'd probably send them there. And guess what? You don't even get a bump for the referral."

The light finally went on in my brain. "I get it. I get it. That's how I need to position the Red River Grill. But I don't really have any gimmicks to feature."

"You don't necessarily need a gimmick," Lucinda said. "The key is to identify what it is — tangible or intangible — that makes the Grill unique. It's all about pinpointing its personality, then conveying it to your customers."

"Any ideas?"

"What about getting some more mileage out of your head-shaving?" Lucinda asked. "Lord knows it didn't improve your looks. It might as well improve the marketing of your restaurant. Thanks to the media coverage, a lot of the foundation has already been laid. People now associate the Grill with great food, great drinks and fun. Capitalize on that."

Lucinda and I spent the next hour or so brainstorming ideas to leverage the exposure my bald head had received. First of all, I'd collect the best photographs of the event — the ones Kate had shot — and place them in the center of the Wall of Fame we were building. It would be an effective reminder of how fun it is to eat at the Red River Grill, and it would also promote positive word of mouth. I could imagine guests saying: "You have to try the Grill. It's that place whose wacky owner shaved off all his hair when the Wildcats won the title."

Being commonly associated with the Wildcats would also be a positive thing — much like having an unspoken endorsement from the team, which would drive business on game nights and nicely complement any promotion we might run. As for a couple of possibilities, Lucinda suggested a "Dean Look-Alike" contest in which we let those in attendance, by the level of their applause, determine the winners. On game nights, we could also devise special offers and discounts for bald-headed guests.

What about T-shirts — the literal component of walking, talking billboards? We'd have to come up with something more clever than the usual logo-on-the-front-pocket approach. Perhaps we could incorporate a slogan into the T-shirt design, one promoting a top-shelf specialty drink: "Home of the Chrome Dome." The so-called "Chrome Dome" could be a frozen margarita with a blue "W" (for Wildcats) etched into a dome of shaved ice.

Before I burst at the seams with marketing excitement, Lucinda added a dose of reality. "Just remember, Dean, that despite all the mileage you get out of going bald, one day you'll probably have to come up with another spellbinder to keep attention focused on the Red River Grill. One way is to make the head-shaving offer every year during the conference tournament. But that could backfire on you. It's hard to recycle old news, especially when the public's always looking for something different."

"No, I don't think I'd shave my head again," I said. "But by applying everything you and others have taught me about *Slam Dunk Marketing*, I'm sure I'll come up with something big. Maybe every month in

the off-season I could offer one month's free burgers —
our new 'Chrome Dome Burger' — to any D.J. willing
to shave his or her head at our place on the air."

"There you go," Lucinda said.

With that, dinner was down to the fortune cookies.
I broke open one of the sugary crescents and pulled out
the slip of paper.

"What does it say?" Lucinda asked.

A smile crept over my face. "It says: 'The person
you're dining with will bring you happiness or success.'"

"I wonder which it will be?" Lucinda said, playfully
deflecting my gaze into her eyes.

Shrugging my shoulders, I answered: "I've got a
pretty good idea."

The next day in my office, located in the back of
the restaurant, I went over the notes recently added to
my marketing notebook.

Talk of the Town
The Figurative Billboard
The Literal Billboard
The Window Seat
Why You?

Afterward, I began to
contemplate how I'd go
about continuing my *Slam
Dunk Marketing* success.
Determined not to be
satisfied with just one big
winner, I figured the
worst thing I could do at
this point was abandon

what essentially got me here — ideas picked up from the effective marketers around me.

One of the best ways to make sure an idea is indeed a slam dunk, I'd learned, is to let another business go through the initial trial and error of execution. Once it's proven to be successful, there's no law against me "borrowing" the idea, tailoring it to fit the needs of the Red River Grill and expanding on its initial success.

I also planned to enlist the help of my employees. Each one probably visited other restaurants in the area three times as often as I could. If motivated, they might keep an eye peeled for winning promotions. I'd reward those who brought in the most promising ideas that Kate and I ended up implementing. A small percentage of the profits might be in order.

The ongoing search for *Slam Dunk Marketing* ideas wouldn't be limited to the restaurant industry. Certainly, service-oriented businesses of all kinds were busy thinking up winning promotions. I'd just have to pay attention when patronizing local retail outlets, grocery stores, car rental agencies, even bowling alleys. You never know what you might find.

The ring of the telephone interrupted my thoughts. It was Coach.

"How the hell are ya, Dean?"

"Not as good as you are," I said. "You've exceeded even your own celebrity status."

Coach didn't buy it. "You're the one that's become a celebrity," he said. "Whatever made you decide to shave your head?"

"Well, Coach," I said. "To be the best, you've got to look your best. And with you as a fashion template, I couldn't lose."

Coach and I, two eggheads savoring victory, had to laugh at that one. What we didn't know was that the biggest laugh was yet to come.

— *"I'd hate to be in the shoes of your competition right now," Coach said. "You're going to blow them away."*

# CHAPTER 10
## THE DOMINO EFFECT

Within walking distance of the Red River Grill is a large stretch of well-manicured lawn, flower beds and old-growth trees, officially called Metropolitan Park but locals know it as "The Met." You can walk a dog there, catch some rays, take a lunch break, whatever suits your fancy. Or, if you're serious about basketball, you can push and shove in the weekend pickup games that take place at the park's asphalt court, where the written "rules of play" mean little or nothing to the participants and the hoops are reinforced with breakaway rims and chain-link nets.

On a bright Sunday afternoon, Coach and I sat next to each other on a park bench near mid-court. We were scouting the talent playing ball in front of us and waxing poetic about our mutual victories — his in the conference-championship game and mine inside the restaurant.

"The thing that gets to me," I said at one point, "is that it's taken me this long to understand what I've been calling the *Slam Dunk Marketing* principles. Imagine where I'd be today if only I had caught on sooner."

"All in good time," Coach answered. "If it were too easy, you'd either take success for granted or be too soft to battle the competition. Adversity makes us more focused and stronger."

"In what ways?" I asked.

"Take the Wildcats, for instance. We lost a few games early on in the season. The newspapers were writing us off faster than a tax deduction, the players were hanging their heads, even my wife wasn't talking to me. Losing, however, was the best thing that could happen to a young team, because the lessons the guys learned strengthened their resolve and enabled them to reach peak performance at the time of the tournament. Teams that peaked too early in the year ran out of steam."

"As always, you've hit the nail on the head," I said. "My resolve to succeed — to get a slam dunk on every marketing effort Kate and I try — has never been stronger or more targeted in the right direction."

"I'd hate to be in the shoes of your competition right now," Coach said. "You're going to blow them away."

Coach had a way of making me brim with confidence. He was also very interested in what I had done to arrive at the *Slam Dunk Marketing* principles. I started at the beginning, telling Coach about the day I overheard a couple discussing the Red River Grill. "Let's not tell anybody about this place," they had agreed. "It'll be our secret."

"It was at that point," I told Coach, "that I became determined to turn around the marketing fortunes of the restaurant. A firm commitment to improve is the first step in reaching *Slam Dunk Marketing* success."

"Makes sense," Coach said. "Then where do you go?"

"Well, the morning after I made the commitment to improve my marketing skills, I went to the Broadway Health Club to work out. That's when I ran into you, Coach, and we hit the treadmills. Your story about the impersonal offer we sent out and the poor service you got when you came in to redeem it convinced me that what the Red River Grill does *externally* to attract customers isn't nearly as important as what it does *internally* to make sure customers come back and bring along their friends. That's the second step — making sure you over-deliver on promises you make in your marketing materials."

"OK, I'm with you. What's the third step?" Coach asked.

"Lou at the Downtown Barbershop taught me the third step, which is to do everything in your power to turn newcomers into regulars. We're already building repeat customers from a mailing list we put together from business cards collected in a fishbowl. We've also established a Wall of Fame designed to make guests feel like stars and want to come back to the Grill again and again to see the pictures of themselves. But the most important thing we're doing — managers and staff — is learning and using guests' names. It's true: People really do want to go where everyone knows their name."

"Step four?" Coach asked, obviously wanting to hear the whole package.

"That would be developing 'One-Two Traffic,' a concept Lucinda was generous enough to pass on to me. Basically it means that attracting new and even repeat customers is not enough. You have to sell them something while they're there — and do it in a way that enhances their dining experience. You have to make sure one sale leads to another and one visit leads to the next. Using video programs and role-play exercises, we're training our wait staff to guide guests through the menu, recommending food and beverage that'll make each visit more enjoyable. Helpful selling is perceived by guests as quality service, plus it increases the Grill's profitability and the servers' tips."

I jumped right into step five, before Coach had a chance to interrogate me about my deepening relationship with Lucinda.

"The fifth step crystallized while buying a dozen roses from Franny at Mother Earth Flowers. As I used the punch card issued to me, she underscored the importance of pursuing short-term marketing strategies only if they help you achieve long-term results. To that end, it's wise not to rely on selling product to more customers but, instead, focus on selling more product to the customers you already have. One way to do that is through bounceback offers, which require customers to come back another time to redeem them."

"This is getting good," Coach said. "Go on."

"Step six involves developing a game plan. Once again, I have to credit Lucinda, who recognized that a lot of business owners — myself included — make the mistake of starting at the beginning when forming a plan. In going from A to Z, however, they often discover in the end that Z stands for zero profits because the decisions made early on didn't support a worthwhile return on investment. The solution is to target a 10-to-one R.O.I. — 10 bucks for every one invested — then plan your marketing ventures in reverse, determining the finish line before the race starts."

"And that's why you attended my blackboard session that day," Coach said. "Because I execute the Wildcats' game plan in the same manner."

"You got it," I said. "And since you brought up the French Revolution slogan 'execute,' I'll reveal the seventh step, which just happens to be *executing* the game plan. The process revolves around backtiming — the art of proceeding in reverse, day by day, to plot every step needed to execute a marketing event. The key is to be complete, but keep things simple. For each day — working backward, remember — we detail only the task, the person responsible for completing the task and the time by which the task should be completed. In essence, it's a daily mini-action plan which forces us to think through exactly what needs to be done to avoid making frivolous assignments."

"Nice idea," Coach said.

"Yeah, but it's all meaningless if you don't finish what you started — or, more important, if *we* don't finish what *I* started. That's the eighth step. I learned the hard way that you can devise a beautiful game plan and take action to execute it from a management point of view, but unless you get commitment and effective performances out of your employees, you're dusted. It occurred to me that salespeople tend to work for commission on product they sell, and often receive motivation in the form of sales contests. Servers and bartenders at the Red River Grill — *my* salespeople — also earn commission, as much as 10 to 15 percent in tips on each guest check they turn in. If they'd just commit themselves to providing customer-pleasing little something extras and building per-person check averages, their tips would dramatically improve, as would the success of any marketing program under way. To sweeten the pot, I now make it a routine to implement sales contests to support any promotion the Grill runs."

"Looks like some of your past experience in that huge corporate bullpen known as the Sales and Marketing Division is finally paying off," Coach said.

"That's what gave me the idea for sales contests," I said. "But to be honest with you, running a successful restaurant is a whole different jar of pickles."

"Yeah, kosher dills it's not," Coach said. "So what's the next step? I guess we're on number nine."

"Nine it is — a principle that came to me after seeing most of the town wearing Wildcat T-shirts, sweatshirts and ballcaps, advertising your basketball program for free. Lucinda calls it 'Walking, Talking Billboards,' which I figured the Red River Grill could use in abundance. The billboard can be literal, as in the case of customers wearing T-shirts, sweatshirts and ballcaps bearing our logo. Or it can be figurative, as in the case of customers spreading positive word of mouth. Either way, the restaurant is better off. To create these billboards, we've decided — Kate and I — to get more mileage out of my bald head, creating fun specialty drinks, T-shirts and promotions that keep the event top-of-mind with customers and potential customers."

"And now, number 10," Coach said. "I'm breathless with anticipation."

"There is no 10," I responded. "Nine — that's it for *Slam Dunk Marketing* success."

"How can you have a nine-step plan?" Coach asked. "That has no ring to it. You have to have 10 steps. It's un-American if you don't."

"Any ideas?"

"Damn right," Coach said eagerly. "And it may be the most important step of all."

"OK, now *I'm* breathless with anticipation."

"You can't rest on your laurels," Coach advised. "I've seen it time and time again. A coach wins a big game or even the conference tournament and gets lulled into a false sense of security. Then — *boom* — he or she falls off the ivory tower. The secret is to keep building onto each and every victory, no matter how great or small. One success leads to another."

"Like dominoes," I said. "You push one down, then the next one falls, and then the one after that."

"All right then," Coach said. "Let's call step 10 the 'Domino Effect.' But there's one more thing you should keep in mind, a principle that ties everything together — all the steps you've related to me today. In the basketball program, we call it A.M.S.I.P., which stands for 'All Marketing Success Is Personal.'"

"What does that mean exactly?" I asked.

"What it means is that it takes personal effort and commitment to reach your ultimate goals. In our case, it's the efforts of the assistant coaches and the players who delight the fans with their performances on the court. It's also the countless people behind the scenes — in the ticket booths, in the concession stands, even in the parking lot — who have a stake in pleasing our customers and generating return visits to watch the Wildcats in action. At the end of the day, however, it's me — and only me — who bears the responsibility for success or failure. I don't take the credit, but I do have to make sure the job gets done. As soon as I get out of the driver's seat, the team bus goes over the cliff."

I understood what Coach was getting at. I had been concentrating on extracting personal effort and commitment from my bartenders and servers, but it's equally important to involve the people behind the scenes at the Red River Grill. From the front of the house to the back of the house, it's a team effort.

"So what you're saying, Coach, is that even the best-laid plans have little chance to succeed without full staff support and the understanding that ultimate responsibility rests on my shoulders."

"That's exactly what I'm saying," Coach said. "If you remember nothing else, remember A.M.S.I.P. — All Marketing Success Is Personal."

As we watched the pickup game unfolding before us, I realized that reviewing the *Slam Dunk Marketing* principles had been a valuable exercise. I'd repeat them often as a training exercise for my managers and staff, kind of a running review. The addition of the 10th step, along with the A.M.S.I.P. principle, also got me thinking about the possibility of joint-marketing efforts with non-competing businesses in the area, which could make the dominoes fall even faster.

One idea I came up with was trading out gift certificates with the city's busiest dry cleaner down the street. I could use his as rewards in my sales contests, and he could use mine to stroke his V.I.P. customers, which in turn would promote the Red River Grill. I could also gain access to his database to locate new customers in my neighborhood, "piggybacking" on his success and

allowing him to do the same with mine. I made the appropriate entries into my marketing notebook.

About this time, one of the players on the asphalt court, recognizing Coach, jokingly challenged him to a slam dunk contest.

"Can't jump that high," Coach said, eye-balling the challenger. "But I'll bet you 20 bucks that Dean here can perform a slam dunk that puts you to shame. I'll even let your friends be the judges."

"Are you nuts?" I whispered to Coach. "You know I can't dunk the ball."

"Just leave everything to me," Coach said.

The street player went first, starting his jump near the free-throw line, then jamming the ball home with a thunderous one-hand finish. His buddies howled with delight, each signaling a "10" with their fingers — a perfect score. You could read in their eyes that they had little respect for me, a short, pudgy former basketball player whose best days were long behind him.

"Now what?" I asked Coach.

Without a word, he walked toward the basket and kneeled down on all fours in the middle of the key, about five feet from the hoop. I immediately knew what he had in mind. Before the competition could protest, I dribbled down the court targeting the small of Coach's back, which would serve as my launching pad. Hitting the mark at full speed, I twisted 180 degrees in midair for a two-handed reverse slam dunk that rattled the backboard and knocked a link or two out of the net.

I don't know if it was the absurdity of my effort or if the street-wise judges were indeed impressed, but they gave me the nod without any deliberation whatsoever. The loser of the contest pulled out a 20-dollar bill and sheepishly handed it to me. My slam-dunk successes were adding up faster than I could have imagined.

"How about a beer?" I asked Coach, holding up the 20. "I'll buy."

No sooner had we started walking, Coach was already two steps ahead of me. The two of us made our way toward what was becoming the most popular restaurant in town. You may have heard of it — it's called the Red River Grill.

## AND ONE MORE THING

This has been the story of how I learned the *Slam Dunk Marketing* principles, which in short order turned around the marketing success of the Red River Grill. They'll work for you, too, no matter what kind of business you're in or what kind of position you hold.

But they're just the beginning. A.M.S.I.P., as it turns out, is just one of the acronyms I've been lucky enough to pick up through my continuing relationships with Coach and Lucinda primarily, but also with Lou, Franny and the many other business owners in the area who've shared their insights. For instance, cast your eyes on these principles:

S.I.M.Y.B. — "Sorry I Missed You, But…"
C.A.M. — "Captive Audience Marketing"
T.I.A.T.A.I. — "Try It And Talk About It"

And:

B.A.B.B.
T.M.T.M.
S.A.M.
D.A.S.M.

My pals and I are really having fun sharing the marketing principles behind these acronyms in seminars and workshops all over the country. I hope to see you in one of our traveling *Slam Dunk Marketing* programs soon.

To start implementing the 10 powerful *Slam Dunk Marketing* steps revealed in *this* book, just turn the page. The action steps presented are taken directly from the pages of my "Official Marketing Notebook," which to this day I carry in my back pocket. It's been an invaluable tool — one that I now share with you.

Sincerely,

Dean 'Baggy Sox' McBride

# Dean's Official

# MARKETING NOTEBOOK

### OK— we've talked the talk, now here's how to walk the walk.

Idea:

DEAN'S
MARKETING
NOTEBOOK
OFFICIAL

Figure ROI
see page 154

Backtime
see page 155

## CHAPTER 1 — IMPLEMENTATION GUIDE
### WHAT'S WRONG HERE?

In this chapter, I made the initial steps toward understanding that there's no secret to *Slam Dunk Marketing* success. Sure, there are steps to follow, mind-sets to adopt, skills to master, customer counts to increase and money to be made. But no book can teach the one thing you'll need most in order to finish strong — a personal commitment to understand the *Slam Dunk Marketing* principles and, more important, to implement them according to the needs of your business.

If you've read every page up to this point, you're well on your way. What follows, chapter by chapter, are the code words I referred to throughout the book and jotted down in my *Official Marketing Notebook*. To this day, I use them as daily *Slam Dunk Marketing* reminders. Along with the code words are detailed explanations and action steps you can use to develop and execute an effective game plan of your own. This section can also help you teach the principles to members of your staff.

I encourage you to make the commitment to give the *Slam Dunk Marketing* approach a try. You miss 100 percent of the shots you never take.

## CHAPTER 2 — IMPLEMENTATION GUIDE
### INSIDE-OUT MARKETING

I learned a lot from Coach during our treadmill workout together, which really started me down the trail of *Slam Dunk Marketing* success. Throughout business school and my many years in corporate America, I was in the habit of seeing the business operation from the outside in. So it's not surprising that I sent out goofy mailers addressed to "Current Residents" instead of real people. I'm lucky I didn't get a stack of nasty letters in return — addressed to "Current Restaurant Owner," of course. At the health club, Coach pointed me in the right direction and I've witnessed the improved marketing results first-hand. Here are the secrets to "Inside-Out Marketing."

- Just as Coach explained in his "Seven Foot Simmons" story, you should avoid promising in your marketing materials what your operation can't deliver consistently. It's impossible to build repeat business if you're in the habit of building up customers' expectations, only to pull the rug out from those expectations once you get the customers in the door.

- It's critical to understand the difference between "external" and "internal" marketing. What you do *externally* to attract customers — from newspaper ads to TV and radio spots — isn't nearly as important as what you do *internally* to get them to come back. Before you waste money on external-marketing schemes, you should invest an equal, if not greater amount, on solidifying your internal marketing, whose principal components are the quality of customer service your staff provides and the marketing message you communicate to customers while they're right there with you.

139

© Pencom International • 800-247-8514

Great Expectations
• Exceed the promise

- Your success rides on your staff's ability to exceed the "Great Expectations" of guests entering your operation. You can start by delivering — over-delivering, in fact — on the promises made in your marketing materials.

- The more you expect from your employees, the more you have to train them. Invest in staff-training books, workbooks, videotapes — whatever equally nifty tools you deem most useful in developing employees who know how to exceed the needs of your guests. Remember: Your employees will gauge how serious you are about customer service by the value they place in your investment in them and their training materials.

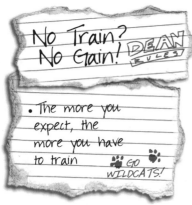

No Train? No Gain! DEAN RULES

• The more you expect, the more you have to train   GO WILDCATS!

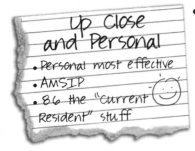

Up Close and Personal
• Personal most effective
• AMSIP
• 86 the "current Resident" stuff

- You have to get "Up Close and Personal" with customers, abandoning impersonal marketing approaches like addressing mailed offers to "Current Residents." Personal marketing is the most effective method of touching customers.

140

# CHAPTER 3 — IMPLEMENTATION GUIDE
## THE STAR TREATMENT

Lou the barber has a way of making his customers feel like stars — including me, Dean, a washed-up basketball player prone to bad hair days and lethal shaves. Serving customers as if they're royalty is a technique that Kate and I, for staff-training purposes, have dubbed "M.M.F.I.," which stands for Make Me Feel Important. That's how customers want to be treated, and I have Lou to thank for sharing this important insight with me. Here are the secrets to executing "The Star Treatment."

- To turn newcomers into regulars, enlist the help of your front-line employees. At regular all-staff meetings, have a heart-to-heart talk with them about the importance of customer service, identifying specific ways to encourage first-time customers to make return visits. Implement the steps the group comes up with. Employees will execute their own ideas better and quicker than ideas forced upon them.

- For ideas that generate repeat business, borrow the tactics Lou employs to build business in his barbershop. Most important is learning and using guests' names, which Lou pulls off in a friendly, natural fashion. It's true: People want to go where everyone knows their name. The easiest way to remember a customer's name is to ask him or her for it.

- If appropriate, purchase a point-and-shoot camera to record the fun times customers have in your operation. Hang the photographs in a public place, honoring your regulars and attracting the attention of your newcomers. Customers will come back to see their smiling face up on the Wall of Fame, and they'll often bring along their friends, too.

The Star Treatment $
• Ask questions and listen
• Wall of Fame

- Do whatever it takes to make customers feel like stars. Learning names and shooting pictures is just the beginning. Take a sincere interest in their everyday lives, try to anticipate their needs as customers, make them out to be the most important person in your store. After all, they're the reason you're in business.

Something Special
• 86 the big things
• Little things add up

- To become something special in the minds of your customers, heed this valuable lesson in generating repeat business: It's not necessarily any one big thing you do, it's a combination of the little things that add up to *Slam Dunk Marketing* success.

- One little thing you can try is collecting business cards in a fishbowl as a way to thank customers for their business. Regularly draw out names of winners and award prizes redeemable at your store. Meanwhile, use the business cards to generate names and addresses for your database. It's also a good idea to stack name-and-address forms near the fishbowl because not everyone has their own card. A lot of businesses use the fishbowl tactic. What can make it a slam dunk depends on what you do with the information gathered.

# CHAPTER 4 — IMPLEMENTATION GUIDE
## "ONE-TWO" TRAFFIC

There's an old saying that goes: "Make hay while the sun shines." The same holds true for marketing. Lucinda explained to me in the sky box at Wildcat Arena that too many business owners, operators and managers bend over backward to get people in the door, but then fail to cash in on all their hard work. The trick is to deliver a one-two punch — attract customers, to be sure, but also sell them something while they're there. Otherwise, you're throwing money down the drain. Here are the secrets to "One-Two Marketing."

No End in Sight
- Get them to come back
- Friends

- The mistake many business people make is to view a particular promotion as an end in itself. Effective marketing, however, isn't a one-shot deal. Your goal should be not only to attract new customers, but also to encourage them to make purchases, enjoy the service or "experience" your staff provides and come back another day — with friends and acquaintances.

One-Two Traffic
LUCINDA
- More traffic
- More sales
- Like a boxer

- Think of a one-two combination of punches in boxing when developing your marketing strategies. Don't be satisfied with just getting people in the door. You have to sell them something while they're there — and do it in a way that enhances their experience.

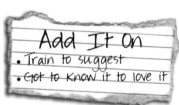

Add It On
- Train to suggest
- Got to Know it to love it

- Add-on sales and upselling are key components of generating "One-Two Traffic." In a restaurant environment, it's important to train front-of-the-house employees, especially greeters, servers and bartenders, to suggest appetizers to go along with the beverage orders, upgrade cocktail orders to include premium spirits, and recommend extras that complement entrees. Also called suggestive selling, the practice is perceived by guests as attentive and better service. Remember: If customers don't know the special deals you offer, they can't participate.

- When adding on and upselling, salespeople should always be polite, not pushy. Their goal isn't to clean out the wallets and purses of customers. It's to enhance the perceived quality of their purchase, whether it's sautéed mushrooms on a strip steak or, in a retail-furniture outlet, matching brass lamps to go along with the end tables.

- It's better to execute a mediocre idea properly than to botch a promising idea. To get the most out of your employees, you have to train them daily, especially in areas that support your marketing endeavors.

147

Bouncebacks
- Repeat business
- Urgency

- Once you've attracted new customers and trained your staff to maximize its service and sales potential, consider using bouncebacks to generate repeat business. Bouncebacks are promotional offerings that are good the *next* time guests come in. Make them compelling and create a sense of urgency to redeem by making them good for only a short time.

GO WILDCATS!

Fix the fish
- Duplicate names
- Cost big bucks

- If you're gathering business cards in the fishbowl to build your database, be sure to check for duplicate names. A lot of regular customers will drop a card in each visit, which can lead to embarrassment and unnecessary costs if you mail to the addresses on every card collected, including the duplicates.

# CHAPTER 5 — IMPLEMENTATION GUIDE
## THE SHORT AND LONG OF IT

What a character Franny Copeland is! At Mother Earth Flowers, she demonstrated how to parlay short-term marketing angles into long-term results, often using unconventional tactics. I especially like the one in which she leaves holiday invitations to visit her store on customers' answering machines. Her emphasis on the personal touch is right on the mark, too. It's amazing to me that Franny, a biker woman wearing a tattoo the size of a license plate, can be such a softy. Truth is, that's why she's so successful. Here are the secrets to maximizing "The Short and Long of It."

"Win 'Em One at a Time."
- Executions
- Rifle approach

Mix It Up

Dean        Competition

- Overlapping promotions
- cross market

- Coach, too smart to make promises he can't keep, always refuses to make predictions about upcoming games. "It's a long season," he likes to say. "We're just focused on winning one game at a time." This is an appropriate mind-set for business operators, too. It's better to execute and analyze one marketing strategy at a time rather than take a shotgun approach to see what works and what doesn't.

- While planning a marketing strategy, incorporate short-term and long-term elements. Don't be content with quick fixes alone. If they don't contribute to potential traffic-building success in the long run, they're probably not worth the trouble and expense.

- Develop a promotional mix. Your well-known happy hour might attract after-work business, but a weekend craft-beer tasting, advertised during the happy hour, could encourage guests to make a return visit — and perhaps stay for dinner and enjoy a leg or two of the beer they sampled. You don't have to strive to get more happy hour guests. Instead, try to get more of those guests to stick around after the happy hour is over. An astute server, overhearing guests discussing an upcoming birthday, could invite them to spend the special occasion at your restaurant. Take advantage of all your opportunities to turn short-term marketing efforts into long-term results.

- Try not to become overly preoccupied with marketing to new customers. It's far more cost effective to maximize the service, sales and profit potential with the customers you already have. They're familiar with your products and services — unlike strangers who have to be persuaded to give your business a try.

- Look for ways inside your store to sell not only your products, but also yourself and your business. Point-of-sale materials can drive purchases, but it usually requires a commitment to personal

151

marketing and customer service to achieve lasting success and generate those all-important referrals, which build business without costing you a cent.

Power of Personal,
Personal, Personal!
• #1 tool — LUCINDA
personal touch
• Call them today

• Don't underestimate the power of personal marketing — whether it's on the phone, face to face or in writing. It's the No. 1 tool you have to create slam dunks. The personal touch can make all the difference, but only if you exercise it yourself and teach it to your managers and staff.

# CHAPTER 6 — IMPLEMENTATION GUIDE
## DEVELOPING THE GAME PLAN

What would I do without Lucinda? Over an uneaten dinner at her place, she underscored the importance of starting any marketing endeavor with the end in mind and using projected return on investment to prepare a marketing budget. Both skills have been invaluable to me ever since. It took a while, but I finally came to the conclusion that I'd prefer to put some money in my pocket rather than in the profit vacuum of an ineffective marketing scheme. Attending Coach's chalk-talk session was also an eye-opening experience. Here are the secrets to "Developing the Game Plan."

B.T.F.P. - Back
To Front Planning

- End results?
- what do we want?
- Short vs. long-term results

DEAN RULES!

- In planning a marketing event or promotion, the mistake often made is starting from the beginning. If you plot the steps from A to Z, however, you may discover that 'Z' stands for *zero* profits because your decisions early on didn't support a worthwhile return on investment. The better approach is to determine where you want to end up before you get going. First, identify your goal — which should have a lot to do with your return on investment as well as your short- and long-term goals — then plan your marketing in reverse.

10:1 and 4:1
- Determine your R.O.I.

- Project the revenue the promotion is likely to generate, then allocate a percentage of it to cover your costs — costs you've determined in advance. If you're after a short-term winner, it's not worth your time for anything less than a 10-dollar return on every dollar invested during the time of the promotion. If, for example, you've projected $4,000 in

154

revenue, you'll want to spend around $400 on the event itself. On the other hand, you could get away with a four-to-one return if you can expect long-term benefits from the promotion — primarily repeat business from customers who took part in the event.

Chalk Talk
• Backtiming strategy
• Specific assignments

• In his chalk-talk session, Coach used the word "backtiming" to describe the practice of planning in reverse. While preparing for an upcoming opponent, he starts with the question: "How are we going to win this game?" From there he and his assistants develop a strategy in reverse, each action step supporting the outcome they want — in their case, a win. They set goals and detail specific assignments for every player. They also assign the right coach to oversee the implementation of each step in the backtimed plan. Your marketing efforts should follow a similar course of action.

Go for
the Goal

- Plan your budget
- 10:1, 4:1 our choice
GO
WILDCATS!

- To reach your marketing goals, make every attempt to make accurate revenue projections for your promotions, then use that figure to determine how much money can be spent on them without derailing your 10-to-one or four-to-one R.O.I. Too often businesses are willing to swallow up-front costs with little or no idea if they'll turn a profit. Optimism is no substitute for intelligent planning.

## CHAPTER 7 — IMPLEMENTATION GUIDE
### EXECUTING THE GAME PLAN

Of course, once you develop the game plan, you have to execute it. I learned the hard way — on April Fool's Day, no less — that you have to stay on top of the details or the details will eat you alive. Once again, Coach's chalk-talk session shed light on how to do all the right things to set up a slam dunk. My only wish is that I had learned these valuable ins and outs long ago. Here are the secrets to "Executing the Game Plan."

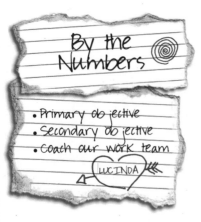

- To orchestrate your own chalk-talk session, use a flip chart and colored markers. The first order of business is to identify the main goals of the promotion you're planning, then work backward from there. Take it one step at a time and avoid the temptation to attempt too much, reaching for the stars and complicating what's reasonably achievable. Keep your objectives within reach. They could be as fundamental as generating enough traffic to produce a 10-to-one return on investment and — no less important — getting those customers to come back for a return visit.

- Write your primary and secondary objectives atop the first page of the flip chart. Then, calling on your own experience and referring to the *Slam Dunk Marketing* principles, identify areas of concern for the promotion, including a complete description of the event itself, external and internal marketing considerations, opportunities for personal marketing and

"One-Two Marketing," components for short- and long-term success, and perhaps a vehicle to collect guest feedback. Determine a budget using the Chapter 6 rules on producing a worthwhile R.O.I.

- The toughest part of executing the game plan is backtiming the essentials of the promotion, including the marketing strategies and tasks that will make it a success. Working in reverse, day by day, plot every step needed to pull off the event. You may discover that deadlines and time constraints prohibit you from doing everything you originally wanted to do. That's the beauty of backtiming — you can spot the holes in your plan before you get in too deep.

- Keep the backtiming process as simple as possible. For each day, detail only the task, the person responsible for completing the task and the time by which the task should be completed. Establishing these mini-action plans is an arduous but rewarding job that forces you to think through each detail of what needs to be done.

- Looking at the multitude of tasks all at once can make the work ahead seem overwhelming. Try to keep your focus narrowed to one day at a time. If done right, the step-by-step planning should keep you on track. Keep a record of the process in your own marketing notebook. It's important to remember what worked well — and not forget what failed.

# CHAPTER 8 — IMPLEMENTATION GUIDE
## FINISHING WHAT YOU STARTED

It took an electric razor buzzed across my scalp to get my brain juices flowing, but I did finally manage to learn the most important element of developing and executing your marketing game plan — it's follow through. Even the most meticulous plans have no chance to succeed without the support and tenacity of everyone involved. It's just like basketball great Bill Russell used to say: "The game is scheduled. We have to play. We might as well win." Here are the secrets to "Finishing What You Started."

Call to Arms
- Commitment of staff
- Communication

- Effective marketing can kill a marginal business. The last thing you want to happen is to attract droves of customers, only to subject them to poor service and bad product. To get the job done on the inside, you have to call on the efforts and commitment of your front-line employees. You have to be not only a manager, but also a marketing coach and teacher, communicating to all what it's going to take to be successful.

Tic Tac Toe
- Sale contests
- Provide rewards

- Words alone aren't enough, however. You have to motivate staff to follow through on the floor, especially under pressure. First determine the kinds of behaviors and levels of performance needed to make the marketing event or promotion a success, then devise sales contests (like Tic Tac Toe) that reward winning behaviors. If you keep it fun and keep your people motivated with rewards that run parallel to your own, you'll produce the win-win you always read about and wondered how it could've happened.

- Include incentives in your efforts to finish what you started. What's the difference between a contest and an incentive? Incentive programs pit employees against themselves. Contests pit employees against each other. A personal incentive — offering to reward an employee for a 10-percent improvement in next month's sales, for example — can be especially motivational for those who tend to fall out of the running in staff-wide contests. Both incentives and contests work. Keep changing them to keep your staff's interest high.

- If you're in the restaurant, bar or hotel business, remind your servers and bartenders that they're on commission, earning 10 to 15 percent in tips on each guest check. If they'd commit themselves to providing customer-pleasing "little something extras" and building per-person check averages, their tips would dramatically increase. Employees who understand what's in it for them to excel at sales and service are bound to do a better job. Capitalize on your built-in incentives.

- Sales contests, incentives and commissions should secure commitment from your staff members. There are many aspects of performance, however, that need not be rewarded out of the ordinary. Often it's appropriate to demand and expect that things be done a certain way. Period. The words "It's your job" should be enough to encourage employees to meet — or, better yet, exceed — the minimum requirements of their position.

- A little motivation goes a long way, especially if you practice what you preach. If you want servers, for example, to recommend a certain high-profit menu item to every table, the message will come across loud and clear if you're seen modeling the way.

# CHAPTER 9 — IMPLEMENTATION GUIDE
## WALKING, TALKING BILLBOARDS

Wouldn't it be great if you could get other people to promote your business for free? Well, Lucinda — my own personal marketing mentor — was quick to explain the possibilities to me. They revolve around a business' ability to delight customers to the point where they're more than happy to spread the good word about its products and services. The Red River Grill may have the best burgers in town, but it takes more than beef and buns to make the restaurant the place to be. Here are the secrets to creating "Walking, Talking Billboards."

- To create walking, talking billboards, you first have to be the talk of the town — or at least the talk of the community in which you do business. Take steps to upgrade your service delivery and go the extra mile to pamper your regulars, so they'll talk about you. Both efforts will help separate your business from the rest of the pack. Also seek out opportunities for free publicity. Get involved with the community, taking part in beautification projects, fund-raisers, assistance for the homeless, etc. It not only is the right thing to do, but also gains positive exposure.

- "Figurative billboards" refer to customers who talk about your business and spread positive word of mouth. If someone were to ask: "What's the best grocery store in the area?" Which one would you recommend? Why? Whether you know it or not, you're a walking, talking billboard for that store — and many others you patronize. Determine what it would take to get similar

166

recommendations for your business, then emphasize those features in your marketing materials, planning sessions and execution steps. Positive word of mouth is the best slam dunk you can create.

- "Literal billboards" can take the form of T-shirts, sweatshirts and ballcaps bearing your company's logo. Customers, free of charge, will advertise your business just because they're thrilled with its products or they think it's cool to let others know they're your fans. Try to develop an environment in which the merchandise sells itself.

- How do you develop that T-shirt-selling environment? Staying busy is a good place to start. Nobody wants to eat in an empty restaurant or shop in an empty store. It sends the message to incoming customers that this isn't a popular place to hang out. Building traffic and generating repeat business will keep things hopping. Even the best operations, however, have slow periods. During those

times, restaurant greeters, for
instance, should seat tables in
bunches, especially near
windows. It creates a better
first impression for arriving
guests.

- Why you? Why not you?
  Identify what it is — tangible
  or intangible — that makes
  your operation unique. Once
  you've pinpointed its
  personality, convey it to your
  customers in a way that's easy
  for them to understand and talk
  about with their friends.
  Positive word of mouth
  marketing is the most valuable
  asset your marketing efforts can
  develop. Every marketing effort
  you generate should also always
  be aimed to generate positive
  word of mouth.

**Why you?**

- Unique points
- Communicate to guests
- W.O.M. rules
- Spoon feed it!

# CHAPTER 10 — IMPLEMENTATION GUIDE
## THE DOMINO EFFECT

If anyone is an expert on slam dunks, it's Coach. In the park, both of us watching a pickup basketball game, he challenged me not to be satisfied with just one success. It should be merely a stepping stone to the next bigger and better slam dunk. The cycle never ends — just like an infinite number of dominoes falling down, one at a time, each reliant on a push from the one that preceded it. The good news is that you don't have to go it alone. When it comes to *Slam Dunk Marketing*, you can get a little help from your friends. Here are the secrets to producing "The Domino Effect."

169

- Once you start achieving *Slam Dunk Marketing* success, don't rest on your laurels. Build onto each and every victory, no matter how great or small. One success leads to another — just like dominoes. You push one down, then the next one falls, and then the one after that.

- The steps in *Slam Dunk Marketing* won't amount to much without integrating the A.M.S.I.P. principle, which stands for "All Marketing Success Is Personal." It takes personal efforts and commitments — on your part and the part of your staff — to reach ambitious goals. At the end of the day, however, it's you who bears the ultimate responsibility for success or failure. So you have to both do it and teach it.

- There's no rest for the weary. Even the best-laid marketing plans have little chance to succeed without ongoing staff and management support. Enlist the help of your employees. If motivated, they might watch out for winning promotions. Reward those who bring in the most promising ideas that you end up implementing. A small percentage of the profits might be in order, or you might even tie the R.O.I. on the project to an employee incentive. Their success is your success — and vice versa.

- Share the *Slam Dunk Marketing* principles with other managers on your staff, reviewing them on a regular basis. What was important to you the first time you read the book might take a back seat to another idea the next time through. Implement the ideas one at a time — or several at once. Before you can say alley-oop, you'll be going in for a slam dunk.

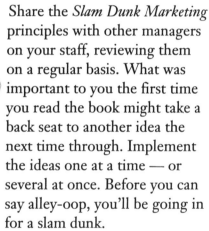

- Keep your eyes peeled for the possibility of joint-marketing efforts with non-competing businesses in your area. By piggybacking on their success and allowing them to do the same on yours, both of you will grow stronger and build traffic faster than ever before.

# Pencom International

# PRODUCTS

## ...to build your bottom line.

### VIDEOS

#### *Service That Sells!*
#### The Art of Profitable Hospitality

The 12 Moments of Truth that made *Service That Sells!* an international success have been updated in this new release of our best-selling video. *Caring Behavior, Precision Service* and *Sales Performance* — the three legs of *Service That Sells!* — will show your staff how to manage the guest experience effectively from start to finish. *Full Service version* **$99**; *Family Dining version* **$99**

Reinforce your *Service That Sells!* training with **Work Smarter, Not Harder!** *Service That Sells!* Workbooks. See description under "Books" heading for more information and pricing.

#### CheckBusters: The Art of Smart Selling

Raise check averages a minimum of 25 cents per person — or your money back. Fun and fast-paced, *CheckBusters* is loaded with tips and techniques that promote sales while enhancing how guests perceive the quality of service your staff provides. **$149**

**CheckBusters Workbooks.** Ideal for a comprehensive program and training retention. **25 for $69.95; 50 for $99.95**

### Heads Up! Tapping into Craft Beer

More fun than a hoppy pilsner, *Heads Up!* demystifies the endless varieties of craft beer on the market, giving bartenders and servers the knowledge and brewing background they need to sell and serve with the best. **$69**

### Pour on the Profits

Teach your staff how to maximize sales and service potential at the bar using "table talk" to break down conversational barriers and "product wisdom" to put guests in a buying mood. **$99**

### The "Sell More" Series

Focus your sales training with the "Sell More" series. Perfect for viewing at pre-shift meetings.

Sell More Beer — **$69**

Sell More Wine — **$69**

Sell More Appetizers — **$69**

Sell More Desserts — **$69**

### Uncommon Grounds: Cashing in on the Coffee Craze

Educate servers in the art of selling and serving specialty coffees. *Uncommon Grounds* explores the ins and outs of preparation, product knowledge and promoting add-ons. **$69**

## NEWSLETTER

### The Service That Sells! Newsletter

Get the edge on your competition for a quarter a day. Service, sales, cost control, leadership, marketing — the management tool you need to run a profitable operation. One-year subscription **$99**, two-year subscription **$149**. Canada **$139** per year. International **$169** per year. Multiple subscription rates available.

## BOOKS

### Service That Sells!
### The Art of Profitable Hospitality

This is it. The best-selling book in foodservice history. More than 300,000 sold. An indispensable resource for restaurant owners, operators and managers committed to profitable hospitality and getting the most out of their employees. *English* or *Spanish* **$16.95**

### Quick Service That Sells!™

The profit-building approach that made *STS! The Book* a best-seller is adapted to quick service in this must-have resource. Speed, accuracy, quality, value, consistency, service, atmosphere, personalization — *Quick Service That Sells!* shows QSR operators how to excel in these critical moments of truth. **$16.95**

### Work Smarter, Not Harder! The Service That Sells! Workbook

The *Service That Sells!* philosophy is distilled into *Work Smarter, Not Harder!* strategies your employees can use to improve performance and productivity.

Versions for Foodservice and Alcohol-Beverage Service **$6.95** each, minimum order of 10 required. *Call 800-247-8514 for bulk rates.*

### Turn the Tables on Turnover: 52 Ways To Find, Hire and Keep the Best Hospitality Employees

Lower your turnover by bringing on the right employees and giving them plenty of reasons to stay. **$19.95**

### Playing Games at Work: 52 Best Incentives, Contests and Rewards

Boost staff morale and productivity with these fun, manageable and results-oriented incentive programs, contributed by readers of the *Service That Sells! Newsletter.* **$19.95**

### Pump Up Your Profits: 52 Cost-Saving Ideas To Build Your Bottom Line

Save a bundle in lost revenue this year with tried-and-true measures to widen your profit margins and narrow your wasteful practices. **$19.95**

### Pour It On: 52 Ways To Maximize Bar Sales

Make the most of your adult-beverage sales and service with this invaluable behind-the-bar tool. **$19.95**

### All for One: 52 Ways To Build a Winning Team

Discover how to choose the right team players, develop team-building skills and unite the entire staff with these strategies. **$19.95**

# www.pencominternational.com
# GET CONNECTED

The Pencom International Website is more than a company snapshot. It's a meeting of the minds, where foodservice operators and manufacturers can:

- Interact in a virtual exchange of ideas

- Take part in hot-button industry polls

- Get Real World Training Solutions

All at the click of a mouse.

Updated weekly, the website delivers free sample pages of the *Service That Sells!* Newsletter, restaurant-tested productivity tools and techniques, exclusive offers for visitors, and links to many other important foodservice sites.

**Hop online.** Every product in this listing — and many more — can be ordered off the Pencom International Website through a secure line. Save time when you know what you want. Get the solutions you need – when you need them. Visit us today at **www.pencominternational.com**